MARIE CURIE

By Beatrice Gormley

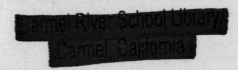

Aladdin Paperbacks
New York   London   Toronto   Sydney

RW 6/07

TO LOIS, MY SISTER AND FIRST FRIEND

ALADDIN PAPERBACKS
An imprint of Simon & Schuster Children's Publishing Division
1230 Avenue of the Americas, New York, NY 10020
Text copyright © 2007 by Beatrice Gormley
All rights reserved, including the right of reproduction in whole or in part in any form.
ALADDIN PAPERBACKS and related logo are registered trademarks of Simon & Schuster, Inc.
CHILDHOOD OF WORLD FIGURES is a registered trademark of Simon & Schuster, Inc.
Designed by Lisa Vega
The text of this book was set in Aldine 721 BT.
Manufactured in the United States of America
First Aladdin Paperbacks edition May 2007
10 9 8 7 6 5 4 3 2 1
Library of Congress Control Number 2006938842
ISBN-13: 978-1-4169-1545-4
ISBN-10: 1-4169-1545-1

CONTENTS

CHAPTER ONE
THE GOLD-LEAF ELECTROSCOPE

In the summer of 1872 in the city of Warsaw, Poland, four of the Sklodovski children were playing "Geography" with their father. They lived on Novolipki Street, on the ground floor of the boys' high school where Mr. Sklodovski was assistant director of the school.

The four beds in the children's room were pushed into the corners, leaving space on the floor for the continent of Europe. Jozef, Bronislava, Helena, and Maria were busy outlining the countries with colored wooden blocks. Their father, Vladislav, moved back and forth among them to oversee the work and give suggestions. He was a short man of about forty, plump but quick-moving. He had a brown beard and he was dressed neatly in a dark suit. Mr. Sklodovski and his children had already marked out the country in the middle, Poland, with bright red blocks. Red was the color of blood, of life, of courage—and, of course, the red-and-white Polish flag.

"Bring me more black, Manya," commanded Jozef. Jozio, as Jozef was called, was the only boy in the family and the second oldest. Manya was the nickname of Maria, the youngest. She hurried "east" with all the black blocks that would fit in her apron.

"Black for Russia, to match their hearts," chanted Bronislava. She was the third oldest, nicknamed Bronia.

Their father was just as caught up in the game as the children were. But at Bronia's remark, he said, "Stop, all of you." His serious tone of voice made them turn immediately toward his broad, kind face.

"Bronia," Mr. Sklodovski went on, "you must be careful what you say." He looked around the room, holding each child's eyes for a moment. "We must all be careful what we say."

"Yes, Papa," said Bronia. The children glanced toward the wall that separated their apartment from Director Ivanov's. The school's Russian director lived just next door.

"Yes, Papa—but it's Saturday, a safe day," protested Jozio. "Director Ivanov is away from the school, and all the students are home for the weekend. There's no one here but us."

"Still," Vladislav Sklodovski told his children, "we can't afford to get into the habit of making such remarks. The next thing you know, when you're walking along the street with a friend, a careless joke will slip out—and a Russian policeman will be listening. He'll grab you"—he seized Jozio's arm—"and question you: 'Who is your father?' The Russians will think you learn such disrespect from me. I'll be fired from my job. We'll have no place to live. Perhaps they'll send me to prison."

"I'm sorry, Papa," said Bronia with tears in her eyes.

"I'm sorry, Papa," echoed Helena, nick-named Hela.

"Yes, I see, Papa," said Jozio. "I'm sorry."

"I'm sorry too," said four-year-old Manya loyally.

The other children laughed. Their father smiled and patted her curly head. But he said, "Even Manya is not too young to learn to be careful."

The serious mood passed, and they went back to the game. "Green blocks, Manya," called Bronia. She was working on the outline of Austria, to the southwest of Poland. Green as the grass in the country, where the Sklodovskis stayed with their relatives in the summer.

"And yellow here, Manya," ordered Hela.

Hela, the second youngest, couldn't outline Prussia, northwest of Poland, without Bronia's help. But she still had the right to tell Manya, the youngest, what to do.

"Blue blocks, Manya," said Jozio. He'd quickly finished Russia. Now their father was showing him where to lay out the Vistula River, which ran through the city of Warsaw. Blue blocks also outlined the Baltic Sea, on the northern edge of Poland.

As the sisters and brother worked on their map, music sounded from another room. Their mother, Bronislava Sklodovska, was playing Chopin on the piano. They heard forceful chords, followed by a prancing bit and a sweeping run. Then the rapid line of notes broke off. The children were used to this, and they didn't stop their play to listen to their mother's fit of dry coughing. But Manya, watching her father's face, saw it tighten.

"Manya," announced Zofia's voice from the

doorway, "it's time to get ready for bed." Zofia, or "Zosia," at age ten was the oldest of the Sklodovski children. She looked at the arrangement of colored blocks. "That's quite a good map!" she exclaimed. "Only, Jozio, the Vistula River winds toward the west a bit more, right there." She tapped a blue block with the toe of one high-buttoned shoe. "But never mind—you have to put the blocks away in a few minutes so that Manya can go to sleep."

Manya hated to stop playing, but she let Zosia take her to the wardrobe to undress her. Manya thought of Zosia as the most beautiful young lady she's ever seen. Golden hair streamed down her back, and she had a quick, graceful walk.

When Manya had her nightgown on, Zosia led her to say good night to their mother. Bronislava Sklodovska was also beautiful, but she moved slowly. She never hugged and kissed Manya the way Zosia did. Mama, thought Manya, was like a delicate china figurine. She could be looked at, but not played with. Mama even ate off special plates, which had to be washed separately from the rest of the family's dishes.

Zosia set Manya down on a footstool beside the piano bench. Smiling at her youngest child, Bronislava smoothed her curly, ash-blond hair. "Sing with me, Manya." She began a lullaby. "Oi lu lu lu lu lu..."

Manya joined in, adding her piping little voice to her mother's violinlike tones. She knew all the verses to this lullaby. The last verse ended, "I have you, my darling—you're what I've prayed for."

Early one morning a few days later, a *droshky*, a horse and buggy for hire, pulled up in front of the boys' high school on Novolipki Street. Bronislava Sklodovska was going to leave her family in Warsaw for a while, to live in a sanatorium. A sanatorium, Zosia told Manya, was a special place where tuberculosis patients could rest and get well.

"This sanatorium is in the mountains, in Austria," Zosia explained. The children had been playing "Geography" again, and she pointed to a spot on the floor just across the line of green blocks. "When Mama comes back, she'll be all well."

Manya put her arms around her oldest sister's legs. "I wish *you* weren't going, Zosia."

Zosia stooped to hug Manya hard. But then she set her mouth in a firm line, as if she wouldn't allow herself to be sad about leaving. "Mama needs me to keep her company and look after her. You and Jozio, Bronia, Hela, and Papa will have each other."

When it was time for Mrs. Sklodovska and Zosia to leave for the train, Aunt Lucia, Bronislava's sister, came to join them in saying good-bye. Mr. Sklodovski climbed into the *droshky* to see them off at the railway station.

Mama and Zosia waved their handkerchiefs as the horses pulled the carriage into traffic. Manya and the other children waved back, watching as the *droshky* rattled off, disappearing among the swarm of carts, carriages, and buggies on Novolipki Street.

"Come," said Aunt Lucia, "we must pray for your dear mama to get well." She took the children to the nearby Church of the Virgin. Manya knelt obediently in the pew beside her aunt and repeated the words of the prayer.

When they returned home, Manya wandered into the study. She gazed at the malachite clock, made from a block of green stone, on the desk, and at the oak-framed barometer on the wall. She came to a halt in front of a glass cabinet. The cabinet shelves held polished brass scales like a tiny seesaw and a glass jar with a brass top and bottom. Inside the jar, two gold-foil leaves hung down from the top. Jozio had told Manya what this thing was called: an *electroscope.* Manya longed to handle it.

Vladislav Sklodovski, who had just returned from the train station, stepped into the study. He sat down in the red velvet armchair next to the cabinet. "So, Manya," he said, leaning forward, "do you like my physics apparatus?"

Manya nodded. "Phys-ics ap-par-a-tus," she repeated. Judging by the look on her father's face, these were important things. "Do they need to stay in the cabinet?"

"Yes, they do," her father answered.

These bright, fascinating objects were not for play. At least, not for child's play.

"These days, teachers are not allowed to give practical demonstrations of physics in the classroom," Mr. Sklodovski added. "Someday it may be allowed again, and then I'll need my apparatus."

"Will you teach me, Papa?" asked Manya.

Her father seemed to like this idea, because the worried lines around his eyes and mouth softened. He answered her seriously, "When you're ready."

Mrs. Sklodovska and Zosia returned from the sanatorium to Warsaw at the end of the summer. Manya was overjoyed to have them home. But no one said to her, "You see? Mama is all well!" In fact, Bronislava Sklodovska was still thin and pale. She still coughed, and her dishes still had to be washed separately. She smiled at Manya like an angel, but she still didn't kiss her, or any of the children.

Manya thought of her mama as the lovely, perfect queen of the family, but Zosia was the one who led the children and thought up ways to have fun. She made up the best stories and acted out all the parts. If the children quarreled, Zosia would settle the quarrel and start them playing a game instead.

In the long autumn evenings the older Sklodovski children gathered around their father's big mahogany desk in the study to do their homework. Their mother sat nearby with her own work: She made shoes and boots for all the children. Her elegant, long-fingered hands cut the leather, stitched the pieces with waxed thread, and hammered the heels onto the soles. "Even though I have to stay inside," she said, "there's no reason for me to sit idle."

The days got shorter and shorter and colder and colder. Then it was Christmas Eve. Through the lace curtains Manya watched the daylight fading and the gas streetlamps beginning to glow on Novolipki Street. "Come on," called Zosia, "it's time to look for the first star!" Jozio, Bronya, Hela, and Manya bundled up against the biting cold and followed Zosia out into the garden.

"There!" Jozio pointed to a shining dot above the rooftops of Warsaw.

First star meant it was time for Wigilia, the feast of Christmas Eve dinner. "First star,

Mama! First **star, Papa!**" they shouted as they trooped back inside.

The family gathered around the table spread with the best white tablecloth. Platters of potatoes, fish, and filled dumplings called *pierogi* crowded the tabletop. Before they sat down to the feast, the Sklodovskis broke the bread of love. This was a special wafer, blessed by the Catholic priest and stamped with pictures of the baby Jesus, Mary, and the angels.

From her end of the table Bronislava Sklodovska beamed at the children. Her gaze lingered on Manya, her youngest. "Vladislav," she said to her husband at the head of the table, "we have so much to be thankful for."

"Yes," he answered. "We are all together."

CHAPTER TWO
FREE IN THE COUNTRYSIDE

The following summer, 1873, Bronislava Sklodovska left for another rest cure. Zosia went with her again. This time the doctors sent Manya's mother to Nice, France.

"It's farther from Poland to France than it is from Poland to Austria, where Mama went last year," Jozio explained to his younger sisters. They were playing "Geography" again, which came in handy for imagining where Zosia and Mama were. Jozio placed a black block on the southern coast of France. "That's the city of Nice."

Manya stood balanced on another black block, the city of Warsaw. "I'm going to Nice to see Zosia!" Running across the floor, she hopped onto the "Nice" block, but her oldest sister and her mother were still far away.

The rest of the Sklodovskis left Warsaw too, for a summer vacation. They visited Uncles Henryk and Vladislav Boguski, Mrs. Sklodovska's brothers, at their country home, Zwola.

Summer in the country was freedom! During the long, hot summer days Manya could run barefoot through the meadows, splash in the stream, and make mud pies. If Mama and Zosia had been there with them, it would have been perfect happiness.

In the countryside, there didn't seem to be any fear of the Russian police. Everyone spoke the forbidden Polish language. In fact, the young Sklodovskis and their cousins marched around the stables, singing the Polish national anthem at the top of their lungs. The tune to the anthem was a *mazurka*, a lively dance.

"Poland has not perished," Manya and the

others sang, "as long as we are alive!" No adults tried to hush them up, or talked about prison. Even Papa sang with them.

The children's favorite place to play was an old linden tree with branches roomy enough for all of them. Although Manya was too short to reach even the lower branches, the older children boosted her up. Sometimes the tree was their ship, sometimes their castle. They took along supplies—carrots and gooseberries— from the kitchen garden in case of a long sea voyage or a siege of the castle.

Manya and the rest were expected to do farmwork as well as play. "The true road to Polish independence," Vladislav Sklodovski told his children, "is through hard work. There is no shame in honest sweat."

The children didn't mind. Grooming the horses, gathering eggs, or helping harvest the grain were all part of the summertime fun.

★　★　★　★

At the end of the summer Manya's family left their countryside paradise. The days were turning cool, and it was time to return to Warsaw and the school on Novolipki Street. "The beginning of a new school year, eh?" said Mr. Sklodovski cheerfully as he led them into their apartment. He picked up the mail waiting on his mahogany desk.

While their father read his letters, the older children opened windows to let fresh air in. Manya gazed around the study, saying a silent hello to the familiar objects. She was glad to see the barometer and the physics apparatus cabinet again. But the piano with its closed lid gave her an empty feeling. She wished her mother and Zosia could have come home too, but the doctors wanted Bronislava to stay in the warm south of France for the winter.

The room had grown silent. Sensing something wrong, Manya turned from the cabinet. Her brother and sisters were all looking at their father. Vladislav Sklodovski, holding an open letter, stared unseeingly over their heads.

"What's the matter, Papa?" asked Bronia.

"It seems—" Their father's voice caught, and he cleared his throat. His gaze shifted to their faces. "It seems I am no longer assistant director at this school. Director Ivanov has downgraded me; I am now just one of the teachers."

For a moment there was a shocked silence. Papa didn't shout or storm around the room, but the look on his face frightened Manya just the same.

"That's not fair!" exclaimed Bronia. "How dare Director Ivanov do that, Papa? You're a better teacher than he is. He can't even write Russian correctly—you said so yourself."

"That's just why he downgraded Papa," said Jozio. He shook his fist in the direction of Ivanov's apartment. "And because Papa's Polish and Ivanov's a dirty Russian."

Manya expected her father to scold Jozio

for speaking his mind about Russians, but Mr. Sklodovski didn't seem to hear. He was staring at the letter again. "Director Ivanov says I am to move out of this apartment at once."

"Move?" asked Hela. "We have to move, Papa?"

"We have to move?" repeated Manya. It had been sad to come back to the apartment without Zosia and Mama, but it was much worse to think that their family couldn't stay. The Sklodovskis had lived there ever since Manya could remember. "This is our home!"

"No. This is the apartment for the assistant director of the school," said their father quietly. "I should never have pointed out Mr. Ivanov's mistakes in Russian grammar. Now I am punished for it." He sighed heavily. "Now we are all punished for it."

During the next few days, Manya found that her father was right about the apartment. As the Sklodovskis' belongings were packed and carried out to a wagon, the apartment became less and less like their home. Finally it was nothing but empty rooms. Manya was glad to run out the front door of the school and jump into the waiting *droshky*.

The Sklodovskis' new apartment was in a shabbier neighborhood of Warsaw, and it wasn't as roomy as the apartment at the boys' high school. Still, once their familiar furniture was in place, it looked like home to Manya. The older children still gathered around the big mahogany desk to do their homework, while the hands of the polished green malachite clock moved toward bed-time. Mr. Sklodovski still sat in his favorite red velvet–covered armchair to read, and he studied the oak-mounted barometer on the wall to forecast the weather.

One evening, after the homework was fin-ished, the children talked about what they would do when they grew up. "I'm going to be a doctor, like Louis Pasteur," said Jozio.

"So am I," said Bronia eagerly.

"But you can't, because girls can't go to the university," said her brother. He didn't say it in a mean way, but Bronia glared at him.

Their father spoke up. "It's true that girls can't study at Warsaw University, or at the University of St. Petersburg in Russia. But Bronia could go to France and study at the Sorbonne in Paris. In our family, no one who wishes to follow a noble ambition like medicine will be denied an education."

"I don't want to go to France," said Hela. "I'm going to be an opera singer."

"I'll be a teacher, like Mama," said Manya. She couldn't imagine anything better than being just like her mother—only in good health.

One afternoon, while Jozio and Bronia were still at school, Vladislav Sklodovski took the barometer down from the wall and set it on his desk. Manya and Hela watched him clean the mechanism and adjust the gilt pointers. "We must take good care of our scientific instruments," he explained. "If we do, they will serve us faithfully."

Manya turned to look at the physics apparatus in the glass cabinet, then back to her father. He nodded approvingly. "That's right, Manya. Those are scientific instruments too, and I take care of them by keeping them away from the dust and smoke."

"When I grow up," said Manya, "I'll be a science teacher." Then she could have her own scientific instruments, and she could handle them all she wanted.

Mr. Sklodovski didn't make as much money in his downgraded job at the school, and he now had to pay rent. He decided to earn extra money by tutoring one or two students from the country. These boys lived with the Sklodovskis during the week.

Mrs. Sklodovska and Zosia wrote faithfully from southern France and Mr. Sklodovski read their letters aloud to the family. "The roses and oleanders are in bloom here," wrote Bronislava, "but I wish I could see your blooming faces instead, my dear ones!" She was proud of Zosia, who was going to a French school in Nice. Zosia was at the top of her class.

Aunt Lucia was eager to hear the news from her sister and niece in France too. "Imagine that, Manya!" she exclaimed. "Zosia is best in her class, even though the lessons are all in French!"

Although Aunt Lucia had four children of her own, she came over often to look after Manya's family. She usually brought along her daughter Henrietta, a mischievous little girl. Aunt Lucia would take the children to church, and Manya always prayed for her mother to get well.

With his wife and eldest daughter away, Vladislav Sklodovski spent even more time with his children. Every Saturday evening was set aside for sharing the great literature of the world. Mr. Sklodovski knew several languages well. He read aloud from Charles Dickens's novels, translating from the English as he went. He also read German and French authors. And he read the poetry of the great Polish poets.

"The Russians have driven our best poets from our land," Mr. Sklodovski told his children, "but their poems are with us, as long as we remember them." He could recite many of those poems by heart. Sometimes Vladislav Sklodovski's voice caught as he pronounced the beautiful words, and Manya felt a lump in her own throat. Her sadness for Poland was mixed up with missing her mother and Zosia.

On Christmas Eve the family gathered around the mahogany dining room table, as they did every holiday. This was Wigilia, the happiest night of the year, wasn't it? But it was all wrong, with Mama's and Zosia's empty chairs.

Manya looked up at Papa, holding the Christmas wafer. He managed a smile. "You know," he told his children, "Mama and Zosia are also breaking the wafer right now. I sent them a wafer, blessed by the priest. And I'm sure that Zosia watched the sky for the first star, just as you did. Now they're thinking of us, just as we're thinking of them. So it's as if they were here with us."

Manya nodded and ate her wafer, but she didn't understand what Papa meant. If she couldn't see Mama's loving smile or feel Zosia's arms around her, they were not here. She longed to hear Mama play the piano, or to see Zosia's eyes light up before she launched into one of her wild stories, but it would be months before they returned, and their absence felt like an ache in Manya's chest.

CHAPTER THREE

STRANGERS IN THE HOUSE

At the end of the spring of 1874, Mrs. Sklodovska and Zosia came home at last. It made Manya uneasy that Mama didn't play the piano as much as before. In fact, Mama often had to stay in bed all day. Still, she was home, and Zosia was taking care of Manya and her siblings again.

In the autumn of 1875, six-year-old Manya was ready to enter the first grade at the Freta Street school, where Hela was already enrolled. That morning, Manya was eager to appear before her mother with her neatly braided hair and her school uniform. The uniform was Hela's from last year, but with a fresh white collar. Manya also wore the new shoes that her mother had made.

"How nice you look, my dears, for your first day of school," Bronislava Sklodovska said to Manya and Hela. "I know you will work hard and make me proud. Give my best to my friends, the headmistress and all the teachers."

Zosia walked with Manya and Hela from the Sklodovskis' new apartment, farther down Novolipki Street, across town to the old section of Warsaw. The way to the Freta Street school led through the Krasinski Gardens, the park behind the Krasinski Palace. The clear blue sky set off the elegant white palace. As they walked along the winding paths, Zosia told Manya and Hela a story about a beautiful princess and her wicked stepmother who once lived in the palace. For Zosia, making up a story was as easy as blowing a soap bubble.

Outside the gardens, Zosia pulled her sisters down the long stretch of Swietojerska Street with a hopping game. Then they rounded a corner, and there on another wide street was the Freta

Street school. Zosia waved at the three-story building with its tiled roof and tall windows. "Here, my gracious ladies, we have a historic site: the birthplace of"—she made a sound like a trumpet—"Zofia Sklodovska, in 1862!"

Manya was nervous about going into the school, but she couldn't help laughing along with Hela. Hela quickly added, "And the birthplace of Helena Sklodovska, in 1866!"

"Ah, gracious lady, you are so right," said Zosia. "But do not forget the most important event of all: the birth of Maria Salome Sklodovska, on November 7, 1867!"

The Freta Street school used to be the Sklodovskis' home, Manya knew. Bronislava Sklodovska had been the headmistress when she and Vladislav married. All five of the Sklodovski children had been born in the apartment at the back of the school building.

Now Zosia led her sisters to the front door, where the headmistress stood to greet all the pupils. "Good morning, Madame," said Zosia with a curtsy. "These are my sisters Helena and Maria Sklodovska."

"Yes, welcome back, Helena," said the headmistress. "And welcome, Maria, to our school. I am delighted to have the children of Bronislava Sklodovska. As headmistress, she made the reputation of the Freta Street school." She turned to Zosia. "I do hope your mother is feeling better."

Zosia curtsied again and murmured a polite answer. Kissing her sisters good-bye, she strode away on her long legs, swinging her satchel. Zosia attended a girl's high school, where she was one of the best students.

Before long, Manya felt comfortable at school. Most of the teachers remembered Manya's mother, and their faces lit up when they spoke of her. As for the schoolwork, it was easy for Manya because she'd already learned so much at home. One summer, in the country, she'd learned how to read almost by accident.

At the time, Bronia, two years older, had been learning the alphabet with the help of cardboard letters. At least, Bronia was supposed to be learning the alphabet, getting ready to go to school. Actually she'd used the cardboard letters to play "school" with Manya. The two girls sat side by side on a bench and pretended to spell out words with the letters.

After a week or so, their mother had Bronia try to read from a picture book. Manya, looking over her sister's shoulder, couldn't understand why Bronia was struggling. The letters in the book were just like the cardboard letters. Only, in the book they spelled out real words that fit together and meant something. Manya lifted the book from Bronia's hands and began to read out loud. It was like a game for Manya, until she glanced up at her mother's astonished face. Something was wrong. And Bronia—Bronia's face was red with shame.

"I'm sorry!" said Manya. She began to cry. "I didn't mean to—only it was so easy."

Mr. and Mrs. Sklodovski weren't angry, but they worried that Manya was starting to read too young. "A good education is much more than just reading books," her mother said. They didn't forbid Manya to read, but they steered her away from it. When they saw her near the bookcase, they urged her to play outside or to join her sisters in a game.

Now, at school, she could read and read.

During Manya's two years at the Freta Street school, the Sklodovskis' apartment seemed to grow smaller and smaller. The parents spoke in low voices about the rising prices of butter and books, and Vladislav took in more and more boarding students. The Sklodovskis and their five children didn't mind sharing space with one another, but sharing with outsiders was uncomfortable.

Hela and Manya had to give up their bedroom.

They slept on sofas in the dining room. The girls had furs to keep them warm during the icy winter nights, but the covers kept sliding off the slippery horsehair furniture—it was a tricky business, trying to sleep and keep the covers on at the same time. They had to jump up at six every morning too, so the dining table could be set for the boarders' breakfast.

When Manya came home from school in the afternoon, the apartment was as noisy as a public square. The dining room was full of the students who came to Mr. Sklodovski for private tutoring. The boarding students went to their rooms to do their homework, but there they chanted Russian verbs or mathematical formulas out loud. Sometimes there was banging and thumping when the boys quarreled, and Vladislav Sklodovski had to settle them down.

On Saturday evenings the boarders left to go home for the weekend and the Sklodovskis finally had the apartment to themselves again. Then the family gathered in the dining room for the weekly poetry readings. Mr. Sklodovski gave his children short history lessons too.

"This poem is by Adam Mickiewicz," he would say. "He writes of Poland in 1812. His descriptions are very beautiful but very sad, because we know that our Polish way of life is being crushed by Russian imperialism."

Listening to her father's mellow voice, Manya's heart ached for Poland. Someday, she vowed, she would do something noble for her native land.

After Christmas 1875, one of the boarding students fell ill and had to be sent home. Then suddenly, in January, Zosia and Bronia fell ill in the same way.

The two girls lay in bed side by side, muttering incoherently from their burning fevers. Aunt Lucia came as often as she could to lay cool cloths on their foreheads. She and Father talked in low tones about "crowded quarters" and "careless boys."

Between teaching his students and caring for his sick wife and two sick daughters, Vladislav Sklodovski had little time for anything else. Jozio kept busy helping his father with some of the tutoring, and Hela occupied herself practicing the piano, but Manya wandered around the apartment at a loss.

It calmed Manya to stand in front of the glass cabinet and gaze inside. The scientific instruments seemed to belong to some different, fascinating world, serene and orderly. Manya almost felt that if she could climb inside the cabinet, she would be in that world too.

Finally there came a day when Manya heard Aunt Lucia say to Papa, "I believe Bronia has turned the corner." Seeing her father's face brighten, Manya knew it meant that Bronia was getting well. "What about Zosia?" she asked. "Has Zosia turned the corner too?"

Aunt Lucia gave Manya a hug, but she didn't answer. Neither did Papa. Manya had a dreadful feeling, as if the floor had dropped out from under her.

Not long after that, Aunt Lucia brought Manya into the bedroom to say good-bye to Zosia. Zosia lay still and pale, with her lively gray eyes closed. Manya timidly touched one of the hands crossed on Zosia's chest. It was cold. Manya burst out crying, and nothing Aunt Lucia could say would comfort her.

Zosia's funeral took place on a bitterly cold day at the beginning of February. Manya heard her mother speaking in the next room. She couldn't make out the words, but she heard her anguished tone. Her father replied, "My dear, you *must* not go out. Think of your health and our other children."

Mr. Sklodovski left the apartment with Jozef, Hela, and Manya, all dressed in black. Manya's black wool coat was a hand-me-down from Zosia. Glancing up at the window, Manya saw her mother's thin shape behind the lace curtains. As the procession slowly followed Zosia's coffin down the street, Mrs. Sklodovska moved from window to window to keep it in sight.

In the summer of 1877, the Sklodovskis took a vacation to the pinewoods near Gdansk, on the north coast of Poland. "The pure air is sure to do us all good," said Bronislava Sklodovska. Her voice was weak, and she leaned on her husband's arm to walk from the bedroom of their rented cottage to the porch.

After settling his wife in a rocking chair, Mr. Sklodovski took Bronia, Hela, and Manya for a hike. Manya drew in lungfuls of the pine-scented air as they walked along the trail. If she could have, Manya would have taken breaths for her sick mother.

Mr. Sklodovski stopped now and then to

point out something interesting in the natural world around them. "Do you hear that bird calling? That's a cuckoo." He urged the children to notice the many different kinds of trees and bushes, or how the branches grew in a pattern, or how the veins in the leaves were like the veins on the back of his hand. "Our world is a world of wonders, is it not?" he said, his face shining. "And the more we understand about it, the more wonderful it seems."

The group turned back toward the cottage as the sun neared the horizon. They paused on a hill, watching the western sky turn orange. Mr. Sklodovski was reminded of a scientific article he had read and he talked to his daughters about it. Hela twirled around, lifting her arms, but Bronia and Manya listened.

"The German scientist Robert Bunsen invented a new way to detect an element," their father explained. "You know that elements are the basic substances of which all matter is made, eh? Now, each element reveals itself through the colors of the light it gives off when it's heated. With Dr. Bunsen's instrument, a spectroscope, one can examine the colored lines of an element. That is how he identified the new element *cesium*, by its sky blue lines." He pointed overhead.

Manya gazed straight up, to where the sky was still blue. "It's beautiful," she said.

"Didn't Dr. Bunsen lose an eye, working in his laboratory?" asked Bronia. "He should have been more careful, shouldn't he, Papa?"

Mr. Sklodovski nodded, a troubled expression crossing his face. "Yes, there was an explosion, and he lost an eye. And he almost died from handling the element arsenic recklessly. It is a poison."

The western sky was now glowing red. Manya asked, "Does another element give off that color red, Papa?"

Vladislav Sklodovski looked down at her,

his face brightening again. "Yes, the element *rubidium*. Dr. Bunsen discovered that element too, and named it for its ruby red."

"It's beautiful," said Manya again. She meant the colors, but also the wonderful secrets waiting to be discovered. In order to find them out, you would have to be clever and brave, and work very, very hard.

CHAPTER FOUR

THE SECRET OF POLISH HISTORY

One early morning in December 1877, Manya and Hela were on their way to school. It was still dark out, and their boots crunched on the snow as they walked with their teacher along the narrow streets. Manya and Hela were now going to a private girls' school run by Jadwiga Sikorska. It was convenient for their teacher, Antonina Tupalska, to walk there with them, because she lived with the Sklodovskis. In return for her board, Miss Tupalska helped manage the household. Tupcia, as the girls nicknamed their homely but kind teacher, taught mathematics, languages, and history.

Tupcia, Hela, and Manya came out on Leszno Street, which was wide and well lit with gas lamps. It was crowded with traffic, buggies carrying businessmen dodged around delivery wagons, and people hurrying to school or work rushed up and down the sidewalks. The light shone on the street signs and shop names, written in the Russian Cyrillic alphabet. That was the law in Russian-occupied Poland.

Mr. and Mrs. Sklodovski had sent Manya and Hela to Jadwiga Sikorska's private school so that they could get a solid education in Polish history and literature. According to the Russian-run government schools, there was no such thing as a country called "Poland." There was only "the Vistula territory," a western province of the mighty Russian empire. Naturally there couldn't be any Polish history, and it was ridiculous to speak Polish, the language of a country that didn't exist, or to read poetry in that useless language.

Manya already knew some Polish history from the songs her mother taught the children and the stories her father told. She knew of the hero Jan II Sobieski, who had defeated the Turks at the Battle of Vienna in 1683. Bits of Polish history were scattered around Warsaw too. There was a statue of the Polish astronomer Copernicus at the head of Nowy Świat Street. In the sixteenth century, Copernicus had informed the world that the earth revolves around the sun. That was the beginning, Vladislav Sklodovski told his children, of the science of astronomy.

Near the Old Town market, a statue of King Zygmunt III of Poland lifted his sword from the height of a stone column. Zygmunt III had made Warsaw his capital city. However, he had not been a wise ruler. The main result of his reign in the seventeenth century had been a series of wars between Poland and Sweden.

And at the north end of the old section of Warsaw, on the banks of the Vistula River, the hulking redbrick Alexander Citadel reminded the Poles (as if they needed a reminder!) that the Russians were in charge. The citadel had been built by Tsar Nicholas, the father of the present tsar, Alexander II.

A short distance from Leszno Street, the girls and their teacher entered the Saxon Gardens. On the other side of this park was Miss Jadwiga Sikorska's school. When they arrived, Manya and Hela went to hang up their wraps. The coatroom buzzed with students, red-cheeked from the cold.

"Oh!" said Manya to Hela as they unbuttoned their coats. "I just remembered, I forgot to memorize that long Schiller passage." She smoothed down her dark dress, the uniform of the school, and straightened her white collar. "Well, never mind—I'll do it between classes."

Hela lifted her eyebrows skeptically. "You'll memorize all that German in twenty minutes? I'd like to see that!"

Their first lesson was in Polish history. At

Madame Sikorska's school, the girls studied the whole saga of Poland, with all its heroism—and defeat. In 1772 the European powers of Prussia, Austria, and Russia had divided up Poland like chunks of sausage. Russia had taken the biggest chunk, including the city of Warsaw.

In 1830 in the "November Uprising," the Poles had rebelled against the Russian tsar, or emperor. Grandfather Sklodovski, one of the rebels, had been captured by the Cossacks, the Russian cavalry. The brutal Cossacks forced their prisoners to march 140 miles to Warsaw, through snow and ice. Grandfather Sklodovski's feet had been badly hurt.

In 1863 the patriotic Poles rebelled again in the "January Uprising." This time it was Uncle Henryk Boguski who fought with the patriots. When the rebellion was crushed, he was one of the lucky ones; unlike the leaders of the rebellion who were all hung from the ramparts of the **Alexander Citadel**, he was dragged in chains to Siberia for four years' hard labor.

Even in private schools, like Madame Sikorska's, teaching Polish history was dangerous. Russian inspectors could pop in for a surprise visit at any time. They wanted to make sure that the children were being taught in Russian, and were only learning the Russian version of history.

However, the mighty Russian empire was no match for Miss Sikorska. Her solution was to teach her students *two* versions of history. There was the official Russian version, in which the words "Poland" and "Poles" were never mentioned. And there was the secret version, full of Polish heroes struggling for Polish freedom.

Manya, even though she was a year younger than Hela, was the best student in their class. For Manya, it was easy to read and speak perfect

Russian as well as perfect Polish, and she had no trouble memorizing two sets of important names and dates.

In the middle of the history lesson that day, a bell rang in the hallway. Miss Tupalska froze, and so did the girls. The two long rings and two short ones were a signal. It meant that the Russian inspector, Mr. Hornberg, was here.

The teacher didn't say a word, but swept the books and papers on Polish history off her desk and into a drawer. The girls swiftly and silently passed their Polish history textbooks down the rows. Four of the girls, the class monitors, bundled the forbidden books into their aprons and scurried out of the classroom.

Meanwhile the other girls pulled needle-work samples from their desks. When the door opened, Miss Tupalska sat at her desk with a bland expression on her lumpish face. She was reading out loud from a Russian book, and the girls were all busily sewing buttonholes.

Miss Sikorska, the director, ushered in a heavy-set man with gold-rimmed spectacles that matched the gold buttons of his blue tunic. He had on tight yellow trousers, and if he weren't the school inspector, the girls would have exchanged secret smiles as he sank into a chair. What if his trousers split? But the girls were too terrified to make fun of Mr. Hornberg.

Manya was the most terrified of all. One of the students would have to recite for the inspector, to prove that Miss Tupalska was teaching the correct subjects. No one wanted that assignment. Manya was the youngest in the class, but she was the only one with a perfect memory and able to speak Russian like a native.

Miss Tupalska gave Manya an apologetic look as she said, "Maria Sklodovska, please recite for our guest."

Manya took a deep, trembling breath. Standing in the aisle beside her desk, she answered Mr. Hornberg's questions one by one. She recited the Lord's Prayer in Russian. She named all the tsars since Catherine the Great. She listed the names and titles of the imperial family. *Please, no more,* she begged silently. Mr. Hornberg looked satisfied. Maybe he would let her sit down now. But, no. Pushing his spectacles up on his nose, he opened his mouth again. "Who rules over us?" he asked.

Manya glanced longingly out the window overlooking the Saxon Gardens, wishing she could fly away so she wouldn't have to answer this shameful question.

"Who rules over us?" he repeated in a louder voice.

Manya thought she might faint, or vomit. She knew the answer, of course, but giving it was as sickening, as humiliating, as it would be to lick the Russian inspector's boots. If she didn't answer, though, Miss Tupalska might be punished. Miss Sikorska's school, which

Manya loved so much, might be closed. The teacher and the director might be sent to prison. It would be all her fault.

Manya forced the hateful words out. "His Majesty Alexander II, Tsar of All the Russias."

The inspector's heavy face spread out in a half-smile. That was what he wanted. He rose, nodded to the teacher, and left the room with Madame Sikorska.

As soon as the door closed behind them, the teacher held out her arms to Manya. Manya stepped forward, and Miss Tupalska took her by the shoulders. Like a general bestowing a medal of honor, she kissed her on the forehead. Manya had held herself together for the inspector by sheer force of will, but now the joints of her body seemed to come loose. Trembling all over, she began to sob.

That afternoon, when Aunt Lucia picked them up at school, Hela told her about the inspector's visit. At home, Aunt Lucia told

Vladislav Sklodovski. But Manya didn't want to talk about it. After tea, she settled down at the dining room table with a book.

This book happened to be a treatise on tropical plants, borrowed from her father's library. But any book would do. When Manya was deep into a book, the world around her faded away. On the other side of the dining room's thin walls, the boarders recited their lessons at the top of their voices. Jozef, Bronia, and Hela had a hard time studying with the racket, but to Manya, it was no more disturbing than a chorus of frogs.

Mischievous Cousin Henrietta was over tonight, and Hela told her and Bronia how Manya had memorized the Schiller passage between classes. "That's disgusting!" said Henrietta. "She ought to be punished for that." She was trying to get a rise out of Manya, but Manya, mesmerized by her book, didn't hear.

Henrietta began to giggle and point at

Manya. She had an idea, which she showed the other girls by carefully propping a chair against the back of Manya's chair. Manya didn't notice.

Bronya and Hela picked up the game, smothering their giggles. Soon they had silently built a barricade of chairs around Manya. The structure was delicately balanced, so that it would collapse if she moved her chair at all.

For several minutes the girls waited impatiently, but nothing happened. Then Tupcia called from their father's office, "Finish your homework, children; it's almost time for bed."

"Yes, Miss Tupalska," Manya's sisters and cousin chorused.

"Yes, Miss Tupalska," echoed Manya without raising her head from her book. She read to the end of the chapter and closed her book with a sigh. She pushed back her chair—and all the furniture around her clattered to the floor.

Miss Tupalska called, "What are you doing?

Stop that monkey business at once!" The other girls howled with laughter.

Manya looked around the dining room dazed, as if she had woken from a deep sleep. She looked from the toppled chairs to her sisters and cousin with a level gray-eyed gaze. "That's stupid," she said, and she left the room with her book.

Bronislava Sklodovska had been sick for so long that it seemed she would go on, always a little sicker and a little weaker, forever. But one spring day in 1878, Aunt Lucia beckoned Manya, her brother, and her sisters into their mother's bedroom.

Mrs. Sklodovska, too weak to sit, was propped up in the bed with pillows. Manya took one look at her father, his face pulled down with grief, and quickly looked away. She fixed her eyes on her mother. Her mother's face was white and gaunt, but peaceful.

Mrs. Sklodovska had only enough strength to gaze at each of them in turn and whisper their names: "Jozef. Bronislava. Helena. And my Maria Salome." She lifted her hand just far enough to make the sign of the cross, blessing them one more time. The next day, May ninth, she died.

After her mother's funeral, Manya went through the motions of living without feeling anything but grief. It seemed that she was doomed to mourn for the rest of her life. In the Saxon Gardens, the sweet scent of lilacs filled the air. School let out for the summer holidays, and then roses bloomed in the parks of Warsaw. But Manya couldn't stop crying.

That summer the Sklodovskis went to visit their relatives in the country, as usual. Uncle Henryk Boguski was excited about his new project, a steam mill. "It's sure to make a fortune, for me and anyone who invests in it," he told Vladislav Sklodovski and the other uncles.

The men were talking on the veranda after dinner one day. "If only I can raise the money to build the mill!"

"How many rubles do you need?" asked Mr. Sklodovski slowly. "I have some money saved."

Manya, perching on the veranda steps, thought Uncle Henryk was hard-hearted. How could he sound so enthusiastic about anything, especially a mill? Her mother—his sister—had just died. Manya got up and went to sit under the old linden tree, out of range of her uncle's voice.

One evening in August, after the Sklodovskis returned to Warsaw, Manya went into Bronia's room to change into her nightgown. Since Manya and Hela had no room of their own, their clothes were kept in Bronia's bedroom.

Manya didn't envy Bronia, though, because Bronia's bedroom was the room that used to be their mother's. Manya wouldn't want to sleep in the bed where her mother had said farewell to the family. She didn't even like to go in the room to get dressed in the morning and undressed at night.

Bronia was changing for bed too, and Manya helped her undo the difficult buttons on the back of her dress. Neither of them spoke, but Manya gave one of her long, shuddering sighs. They changed places, and Bronia began to unbutton Manya's dress. Both their dresses were black, of course, since they were in mourning for their mother. The official mourning period lasted a year.

Bronia's firm voice startled Manya out of her gloom. "Maria Salome," she said, "we need to think of Papa."

"Papa?" It hadn't occurred to Manya that their father might need her attention. Brushing the tears from her face, she made an effort to understand what her sister meant. "You mean, because he's lost . . . Mama."

"Yes," said Bronia. She pulled Manya's dress over her head and shook the wrinkles out. "He never smiles anymore. He picks up a paper, looks at it, and puts it down again as if he has no idea what to do with it. He needs our help."

Turning, Manya faced her sister in surprise. Could a young daughter really be expected to help her father? Bronia seemed to have turned into a grown person overnight.

"The only thing that will help Papa," Bronia went on, taking her sister by the shoulders, "is for us to show him that we'll do well in spite of everything. Now that Mama's gone, Papa only cares about us. Mama's last wish, you know, was that all of us have the very best education."

Manya did know that. Ever since she could remember, her mother and father had been teaching the children something or other, supervising their homework, urging them to do well in school. How Mama's wasted face had beamed at her when she heard that little Manya was the top student at Jadwiga Sikorska's school!

Returning her sister's direct gaze, Manya nodded. The two sisters said nothing more, but Manya went to bed in a different frame of mind. That night, she didn't cry herself to sleep under her fur blankets. She lay awake for a while, thinking about what she might do. She *would* help Papa and she *would* honor her mother's wishes.

CHAPTER FIVE
GYMNASIUM NUMBER THREE

In the fall of 1878, Manya entered a gymnasium, a high school that prepared students for the university. The school, run by the Russians, was the only kind of school in Warsaw that could give an official diploma. Bronia was attending the same school, and Jozio was at a high school for boys. They were both doing very well.

When Manya had told her father that she wanted to transfer to Gymnasium Number Three, Vladislav Sklodovski looked worried. "No, no, Manya. You like Madame Sikorska's school, don't you? I thought you felt at home there, you and Hela."

"I need to get an official diploma, Papa," said Manya matter-of-factly. "It's the only way. Hela doesn't need a diploma because she's going to be a musician. But I'm going to be a teacher, like"—she choked on the words—"like Mama." Taking a breath, she went on. "The sooner I start at the government school, the better."

Her father took both of her hands and gazed at her, his eyes bright with tears. Manya felt a pang. Had Papa, too, been crying himself to sleep every night?

Mr. Sklodovski said, "Brave little Manya! You've chosen a noble calling. This is the hope of our nation, to educate our youth. Very well, then, my dear."

So Manya was enrolled at Gymnasium Number Three. The school was on the far side of the Krakowskie Przedmiescie, the main street of Warsaw, next to the Church of the Visitation Sisters. Bronia's brown uniform from last year was mended and shortened for Manya to wear.

At Jadwiga Sikorska's school, the teachers and students lived in fear of a surprise visit from the Russian inspector. But at least the teachers and students trusted one another, and the teachers at Miss Sikorska's, like the ones at the Freta Street school, were friends of Bronislava Sklodovska's. They treated Manya and Hela like members of their family.

At Gymnasium Number Three it was quite different, as Manya knew from Bronia's remarks. Many of the teachers had been hired because they were loyal to the Russians, not because they could teach well. Even among the students, Bronia warned, you had to be careful whom you trusted. On Manya's first day, the girls in the coatroom eyed one another uneasily, as though they were all thinking the same thing.

The first government school teacher Manya met was Miss Mayer, the home economics teacher. Miss Mayer was a short woman with shiny little eyes like a ferret. She didn't smile at any of the girls, but when her gaze fell on Manya, she scowled.

After the teacher had taken attendance, she called Manya up to the front of the classroom. "Maria Sklodovska, why isn't your hair properly combed?" she demanded.

Surprised, Manya put a hand up to her braids. "I combed it this morning, Miss Mayer."

"Kindly do not answer me back," snapped the teacher. She made Manya unbraid her curly hair, and Miss Mayer herself combed it and rebraided it in front of all the students. But as she examined her handiwork with Manya's hair, the teacher's frown deepened. "What is the matter with your hair? It won't stay in the braids properly."

"It's always been very curly, Miss Mayer," said Manya. Her tone was perfectly polite, but she smiled a little when her face was turned away from the teacher. As she looked around the classroom she noticed some girls smiling back, and one actually winked at her!

Later, as the students were on their way

to German class, Manya felt an arm link with hers. The girl who'd winked whispered in her ear, "What's the matter with *your* hair, Miss Mayer? It's so greasy!" Manya felt a giggle bubbling out of her throat. At least there was one friendly person at Gymnasium Number Three. Her name was Kazia, it turned out.

Within a few days, Kazia discovered that her home, an apartment in the Blue Palace at the edge of the Saxon Gardens, was on Manya's route to school. "Come by tomorrow morning and pick me up," she urged Manya. "Not the front entrance of the palace—walk around to where you'll see a bronze lion, and go into the courtyard." Kazia's father was librarian to the count who owned the palace.

So Manya and Kazia began walking to school together every day. The next week, Kazia invited Manya home for tea. Manya was delighted. In October, it was nearly dark by the time school let out, and she hated to return from the grim, dreary school to the Sklodovskis' crowded, noisy apartment.

Kazia's home, on the other hand, was blissfully peaceful. Her mother served tea with bread, butter, and three kinds of jam, and a dessert of chocolate ices. The girls did their homework uninterrupted in Kazia's bedroom. As Manya said good-bye, Kazia's mother gave her a hug and called, "Come back soon, dear!"

One afternoon, as Manya and Kazia were crossing the broad expanse of Saxon Square, Kazia paused in front of the obelisk. The bronze obelisk had been erected by the Russian government after the November Uprising, the Polish rebellion of 1830. It bore an inscription in Russian lettering: "To the Poles faithful to their Sovereign." That sounded very noble, unless you knew that the Sovereign was the Russian tsar. The nearby Saxon Palace, with its graceful rows of pillars, now served as the Russian military headquarters in Warsaw.

Kazia looked at Manya with her head on one side, challenging her. "I don't know what you think of 'Poles faithful to their Sovereign,' but here's what I think." Glancing around as if someone might stop her, she walked up to the obelisk and spat on it. Stalking back to Manya, she stared into her eyes. "*That's* what I think."

Manya felt a surge of joy. "Really? Well, here's what *I* think." She skipped up to the obelisk, dodged between the stone lions that guarded it, spat on the bronze, and skipped back.

Linking arms with a grand gesture, the girls sauntered out of the square and along the border of the Saxon Gardens. Manya hadn't felt so lighthearted for a long time.

Now Manya and Kazia understood each other perfectly: They were both Polish patriots. It became their tradition to stop in the square every day after school and spit on the obelisk. Sometimes Russian troops were drilling on the square because their barracks were right there. On those days the girls would be extra careful.

Vladislav Sklodovski had the same passion for science that he had for Polish poetry. He read scientific journals eagerly, keeping up with the latest developments. He wanted to share his knowledge with everyone, and he sometimes wrote articles explaining the scientific findings in terms that the general public could understand.

One evening in the spring of 1880, Jozio, Bronia, Hela, and Manya were gathered around the dining table with their homework, as usual. Manya opened her science notebook and showed her father a page of rows and columns of chemistry symbols. "Papa, this is the table of the elements you told me about. My science teacher, Mr. Slosarski, drew it on the blackboard for us to copy. But he didn't explain it."

"Professor Mendeleev's periodic table of the elements." Vladislav Sklodovski's tired face lit up. "What a genius! He discovered this way of organizing the elements to show how they are related to one another."

Manya knew that elements were the building blocks of all matter, the basic substances of which everything else was made. Water, for instance, was made of the element hydrogen combined with the element oxygen. Table salt was made of the element sodium combined with the element chlorine. The smallest particle of an element was an atom.

"You see," Mr. Sklodovski explained to Manya, "Professor Mendeleev grouped the elements in rows across by their atomic weights." He put a finger on the top left corner of the table. "Hydrogen. The lightest element, with an atomic weight of one." He slid his finger across the table to the lower right corner. "While uranium, the heaviest known element, has a weight of 239. And, behold, the columns up and down have arranged themselves into elements with similar properties!"

"What about the blanks in the table?" asked Manya. She pointed to the column that included helium, neon, and argon. "In the inert gases, for example."

"Ah. Those are the elements that haven't been discovered yet, according to Professor Mendeleev." Vladislav Sklodovski's face was positively glowing. "And he is being proved right, for the blanks are being filled in, one by one." He tapped the symbol Sc. "Last year—I'm sure you heard me remark on it—a group of Swedish scientists discovered *scandium*."

Manya did remember. What an honor for a scientist, to name a new element after one's own country!

"And only five years ago," Jozio put in, "a French scientist discovered *gallium*." He pointed to Ga on the table of elements. "Speaking of science, Papa, my physics teacher says I have a good chance at the gold medal." Jozio would graduate from his gymnasium next spring. At the government schools, the top student in each graduating class was awarded a gold medal.

Vladislav Sklodovski nodded approvingly. "That will stand you in good stead when you begin studying at the university here. Later, I hope you'll have a chance to study in Saint Petersburg, where Dmitri Mendeleev is a professor of chemistry. The man is a genius."

Bronia had been sitting silently during this conversation, with a brooding look on her face. Now Mr. Sklodovski seemed to become aware of her. "And our Bronia, if she keeps on with her excellent work, will very likely bring home a gold medal the year after Jozio."

Bronia smiled at her father, but only faintly. Manya was puzzled. Could it be that Bronia was doing poorly in some class and hiding it from Papa?

At bedtime, Manya asked her older sister, "Don't you think you'll win the gold medal in your class?"

Bronia frowned. "I might. Who knows?" She was already in her nightgown and brushing her hair.

"But you looked unhappy when Papa talked about it."

Bronia hung her head down to brush the hair at the back of her neck. She didn't answer for a moment, and Manya couldn't see her expression. Finally she straightened with a toss of her head. "The gold medal won't do me much good if I can't go to medical school."

"But you can," said Maria. "Not here in Warsaw, but you can study in France, or in Switzerland."

"Yes, that was Papa's plan. Then, after Mama died, he invested in Uncle Henryk's mill."

69

Manya vaguely remembered that Uncle Henryk Boguski had built a mill in the countryside a few years ago. She'd been sunk in grief for her mother at the time, and she'd forgotten about it. But she realized now she'd heard Papa and Aunt Lucia talking about the mill in grim tones just the other day. "Papa put some money into the mill?"

"He put *all his savings* into the mill," said Bronia. "And the mill has failed. Papa lost all his money."

"All his money?"

"Yes. That money was to pay for our education." Bronia bit her lip. She looked, Manya thought, like someone who has just had a door slammed in her face.

"Oh, Bronia!" Manya tried to think of something cheerful to say. "Perhaps he'll have more savings by the time you graduate."

"No, he won't. Every teaching job he gets is worse than the last one—haven't you noticed that? The Russians really don't want him teaching in their schools at all." Wiping her eyes with the cuff of her nightgown sleeve, Bronia abruptly turned toward Manya. "Whatever you do, don't mention this to Papa! Swear that you won't. He feels dreadful about it as it is."

CHAPTER SIX

MANYA'S FIRST GOLD MEDAL

Bronia did win a gold medal when it was her turn to graduate from high school. And Manya did keep her promise not to say anything to her father about the lost savings. No complaints—not even any questions. From time to time Vladislav Sklodovski would groan, "What sort of a father am I?" He would give a heavy sigh. "My children, who deserve the finest educations—all the money for them is gone, lost."

Then Manya would say, "Don't worry, Papa. We can work and save our own money."

Bronia would add cheerfully, "Of course we can. Just yesterday I met a lady, a friend of a friend of Aunt Lucia's, who might have her daughters come to me for French lessons."

And Hela would chime in, "You certainly don't have to worry about me! I never wanted to go to the university in the first place."

Bronia didn't have much time to give lessons because she was managing the household now. While Bronia was still in school, Mr. Sklodovski had hired a series of housekeepers. But these women tended to be unpleasant or nosy, or both. It was much nicer for the Sklodovskis to have Bronia cooking, shopping, and keeping the household accounts. She also supervised the hired help who cleaned and did laundry for the family and the boarding students.

In March 1881, Manya picked up her friend Kazia on her way to school, as she did every day. When the girls hurried across Saxon Square, Manya pointed to the flag with the black, gold, and white stripes flying from the top of the Saxon Palace. "Look, the Russian flag's at half-mast."

At Gymnasium Number Three, they found out why the flag was flying low. After the students were gathered in the chapel, the head of the school made a special announcement. "Today we in the Vistula territory mourn as the people mourn all across the Empire. Tsar Alexander II has been foully murdered by a terrorist's bomb."

Manya and Kazia didn't even need to exchange glances. Each one knew exactly how gleeful the other felt about the news. During the break, Manya pulled Kazia into an empty classroom and shut the door. They joined hands and whirled around and around. Manya began to hum the Polish national anthem. She didn't sing out loud, but the words rang in her head, as she knew they rang in Kazia's: "Poland exists, as long as we are alive!"

The girls began to dance the *mazurka* steps to the tune of the anthem. Faster and faster they hummed and danced, laughing giddily but keeping the beat. They hardly heard the classroom door opening.

"What is the meaning of this improper behavior?" Miss Mayer stood in the doorway, glaring at them from under her coronet of greasy braids.

"Nothing, Miss Mayer," gasped Kazia.

"We were only practicing steps for dance class, Miss Mayer," said Manya. She was out of breath too.

"Dance steps!" hissed Miss Mayer. "I know what you were doing. You may wipe that scornful smile off your face, Maria Sklodovska. As if you have the right to look down on me!"

Manya was honestly surprised. She wasn't tall, compared with the other girls in her class, but Miss Mayer was so tiny that the top of her head only came up to Manya's chin. "Why, I can't help looking down on you, Miss Mayer."

Miss Mayer's beady eyes flashed, but she seemed too shocked to answer. Kazia nudged

Manya out of the room and on toward their next class. As soon as they were out of Miss Mayer's earshot, Kazia exclaimed, "Did you see her face when you said, 'I can't help looking down on you'? *Hee, hee!* You had her there."

"I honestly didn't mean to be rude," said Manya. "It's just the truth."

Manya found out later that a Pole had set off the bomb that killed Alexander II, killing himself as well. "He must have been a very brave man," she said to her father.

Vladislav Sklodovski shook his head. "Brave, maybe, but not wise," he said. "Violence only results in more violence. And one tyrant is easily replaced by another."

As much as Manya hated going to a Russian school, she'd come to enjoy being in high school because she took so much delight in learning. She loved all her subjects: mathematics, science, German, French, and even Russian literature. **The science** classes were frustrating, though, because the Russians did not allow laboratory work.

Her father sympathized. "How can one really learn without doing experiments to see what happens? After all, that is how scientists test their ideas. And that is the way scientific facts are proven."

On a spring morning in 1883, Manya and Kazia arrived at school with nothing serious on their minds. New green leaves softened the look of the chestnut trees in the Saxon Gardens. The girls were looking forward to a dance class that night. They weren't allowed to dance with boys because they were only fifteen and still in school, but it would be fun to watch Bronia, Hela, and Kazia's older sister dance. And from their chairs on the sidelines, Manya and Kazia could gossip freely about the boys.

Outside the school entrance, Manya and

Kazia ran into a friend. "Leonie!" exclaimed Manya. "What's the matter?" The other girl's eyes were red and puffy, and she looked as though she'd slept in her clothes.

"It's my brother. They arrested him. My older brother—the police came and dragged him away." Leonie gulped. "He was involved in a conspiracy against the Russian government. Someone betrayed him."

"Oh, Leonie." Manya squeezed her hand, and Kazia put an arm around their friend. "Perhaps they're only giving him a good scare and then they'll release him?" Manya suggested.

Leonie turned her face away, so they could barely hear her answer. "They're going to hang him tomorrow," she whispered.

Manya and Kazia didn't go to the dance class that night, and neither did their older sisters. They asked their parents for permission to stay with Leonie all night.

"By all means, go comfort your poor friend," Mr. Sklodovski said to Bronia and Manya. "Ah, me! Her parents must be heartbroken. I was afraid something like this would happen, with the Socialists firing up the university students. The Russians are glad to have an excuse to punish someone."

That bleak night and the following dreadful morning cast a shadow over the rest of the spring. At school, whenever Manya felt her spirits lift the least little bit, she caught sight of Leonie in her black mourning dress. At home she found herself looking sideways across the breakfast table at Jozio, spreading butter and jam on his bread. Surely *her* brother could never be dragged away by the police and hanged?

But obviously, terrible things *could* happen, and some of them had already happened to Manya's own family. Their darling Zosia had been seized and slain overnight by typhus. And Bronislava Sklodovska, the most righteous person

Manya could imagine, had endured a slow death from tuberculosis. Before their eyes she had suffered as horribly as any prisoner of the tsar's police.

Manya was haunted by gloomy thoughts. The only way she could find relief from them was to study, study, study. The harder she pushed her mind, the calmer she felt. While she was learning, at least, she was free.

Eventually the long, warm days of June came to Warsaw. At Gymnasium Number Three, Maria Sklodovska was the top student in the graduating class of 1883. She wore her best black dress, with a corsage of roses at her waist, to the ceremony. Superintendent of Education Apushtin congratulated her and presented her with the gold medal.

The next day Manya said, "Now I can help you with the housekeeping, Bronia." She knew that her sister needed more free time. Bronia wanted to attend the "Flying University," a secret underground system of classes that were being offered in Warsaw.

In Russian-occupied Poland, it was forbidden for women to attend the university. Only a few Polish women could go to France or Switzerland to study. Most of them didn't have the money, or their parents wouldn't let them live abroad. So the women of Warsaw had organized their own "university." They offered courses in anatomy, natural history, and sociology. There were lectures—but no laboratory classes—on the latest developments in physics and chemistry.

Manya did try to help Bronia for a week or so, but something was wrong. She felt utterly drained and barely had the energy to get dressed in the morning. Hela or Bronia would often catch her sitting and staring into space, with tears running down her cheeks. The family dog, Lancet, tried to cheer her by shoving his muzzle into her hand.

Manya began to notice her father looking at her with worried eyes. Once, she came across a half-written letter from him to Jozef, and her own name jumped off the page. "Our Manya takes things so to heart—I am worried about her health."

One day at the end of June, Vladislav Sklodovski took his youngest daughter aside. "Manya dear. With the advice of your aunt Lucia and the rest of the family, I have come to a decision. I am sending you to the country for a year of rest."

"Oh, no," Manya protested. "How could I do nothing when you and the others all work so hard?" The truth was, the idea of doing nothing terrified her.

"There is something poisonous in the air, in the city," Mr. Sklodovski went on as if Manya hadn't spoken. "You are sensitive, my dear, and the overwork and strain have been too much for you. But our native land has great healing powers." He spoke quietly, but his eyes flashed. "Our Polish land has been here since long before the Russian troops marched into Warsaw, and it will be here long after they leave. You'll see—things will seem quite different to you once you breathe the country air and live among country people."

But what about the years of humiliation and drudgery that her father had endured trying to make a living for his family? Didn't he deserve a healing time now that his brown beard had turned gray? Manya's throat hurt to think of it. "Papa! I will pull myself together, I promise. I've been selfish."

"Not a word more." Her usually mild-mannered father held up a hand to stop the discussion. "It's all settled. First, you will spend July at Zwola with the Boguskis. You will leave tomorrow."

Manya opened her mouth to protest again, but Mr. Sklodovski went on quickly, "And you'll take Lancet along. Such a large dog needs room to run around."

"I suppose he'll be happier in the country," said Manya, gazing fondly at the brown pointer. At the moment, his front half was hidden by the sofa as he chewed on something.

"*I'll* be happier with him in the country," said Hela, pulling a tattered slipper away from the dog.

"So will I," said Bronia, rescuing a vase from Lancet's wagging tail.

CHAPTER SEVEN

THE ENCHANTED YEAR

Riding the train out of Warsaw, Manya wondered what she would do with herself during this year when she was forbidden to study or work. Then, as the city vanished from view, she gradually stopped worrying. She simply gazed out the window at the land: fields of grain, woods, now and then a windmill or a church spire.

Manya had gone to the country every summer since she was a baby, but it was different this year. Maybe because of what her father had said, she saw the Polish landscape in a new light. All around her, the plains stretched out as far as she could see. Their vastness dwarfed the little towns through which the train rolled.

Warsaw, Gymnasium Number Three, and the troops drilling in Saxon Square all seemed very far away.

At the end of the train journey Manya climbed into a wagon and rode deeper and deeper into the heart of Poland. The wagon jogged over the ruts in the dirt roads at a leisurely pace. They passed men plowing the fields with oxen and women driving their flocks of geese to market. Manya felt herself sinking into the slow, peaceful pace of country life.

The first morning at Zwola, Manya lay in bed and watched the curtains of her bedroom window ruffling in the breeze. The air carried a midsummer scent of hay and ripening fruit. What would she do today? Maybe she wouldn't get up until ten o'clock. Maybe she'd eat a big plate of wild strawberries for breakfast.

As the summer days slid by, Manya settled in among the cousins and the other guests in Uncle Vladislav and Uncle Henryk Boguski's manor houses. There was plenty to do, but nothing that really had to be done. Supposedly Manya had been invited to Zwola to tutor one of the young cousins, a lively little boy, in French. That took all of one hour per day. Then she had time for important things, like drawing a sketch of her dog, Lancet.

Uncle Henryk loved to entertain, and he'd invited all sorts of interesting people: artists, musicians, actors. Manya's older cousin Josef Boguski, who was studying chemistry, was also at Zwola that summer. Josef took Manya rowing on the stream, and they had silly boat races with the other young people.

In the evening there were dramatic readings and concerts. Uncle Henryk himself was a fine violinist. All of the guests seemed to be talented, and some of them were famous.

"The actor Josef Kotarbinski is here!" Manya wrote to her friend Kazia one morning. All the girls had a crush on the handsome actor. "But he's leaving tomorrow." She drew a sad face and a line of tears in the margin of the page. "I have to go pick wildflowers to make him a wreath."

Manya and the other girls spent hours weaving a beautiful wreath for the actor. Driving off in the carriage, Kotarbinski set the wreath on his head, making a comical face from under the cornflowers and poppies. The girls giggled and cheered.

Again and again that summer, Manya caught herself laughing. Had it really been so long since she had felt such joy? She laughed when she swung high on the swings under the willows by the stream. She laughed with her young cousin, teaching him French verbs. She laughed at Lancet as he chased geese into the pond and the geese chased him out again.

Most of the time Manya didn't think much

at all. But when she did, she was amazed at herself. "I can't believe geometry or algebra ever existed," she wrote Kazia. "I feel incredibly stupid. Sometimes I laugh all by myself, and I contemplate my state of total stupidity with genuine satisfaction." She read a little, but no great literature—only the shallow-minded novels the guests at Zwola were passing around.

Toward the end of the summer, Manya traveled southeast to Zawiepryzce, Uncle Xavier Sklodovski's estate near Lublin. Uncle Xavier, who was really a cousin of Manya's father, ran his estate a bit more strictly than the Boguskis.

Still, no one expected Manya to do much of anything. Her one duty was to practice her riding skills. Uncle Xavier kept a large stable of horses, and all the guests were expected to ride. So Manya put on a pair of borrowed riding breeches and galloped across the plains with the hunt.

Soon after Manya arrived at Uncle Xavier's, it was time for Dozynki, the harvest celebration. The peasants dressed in their most colorful costumes and walked up past the ruined castle to the manor house, singing and playing instruments. They brought wreaths made from the corn and wheat they'd harvested.

Watching with the other guests, Manya cheered as the peasants presented Uncle Xavier, lord of the manor, with a loaf of fresh-baked bread. Then Uncle Xavier, with great ceremony, gave each worker a slice of the bread. Everyone sang, danced, and then sat down to a harvest feast on the lawn. This was the real Poland, Manya felt, looking down the banquet table. She belonged to it with all her soul.

In the autumn Manya and Lancet traveled farther south to Skalbmierz, in the foothills of the Carpathian Mountains. Her jolly uncle Zdzislav Sklodovski lived there with his hospitable wife and their three lively daughters. Manya would spend her sixteenth birthday with them.

Manya was fascinated with this landscape, which was entirely different from the rest of Poland. Instead of the endless plains, here were mountainsides covered with towering fir trees, capped by snowy peaks. Manya was also fascinated with Uncle Zdzislav's wife, Maria Rogowska. She had never met such an independent woman.

Instead of managing the household and family as Polish wives were expected to do, Aunt Maria managed her business enterprises. She had started a lace-making school and a furniture factory. Of course Manya's own mother had been the very capable director of a school, but Mrs. Sklodovska had always dressed and behaved like a perfect lady. Maria Rogowska, a tall, beautiful blonde, not only smoked and drank with the men but dressed like them, in trousers and a jacket.

Maria Rogowska might not have been interested in pretty dresses or dancing, but her daughters certainly were. "Have you ever been to a *kulig*?" Cousin Antonia asked Manya the first morning. "It's a sleigh party." Antonia was seventeen, a plump girl with shiny dark hair and pink cheeks like a doll. Manya shook her head. "No? Oh, Manya! Just wait! There's one next Saturday."

"Or rather," Cousin Hania chimed in, "you can't just wait, because we need to bake cakes for the feast." Hania, Manya's age, was taller than her older sister, and when she was excited, she waved her hands as she talked. "Of course you need to get your peasant costume ready. We'll help you. Can you do fine embroidery? Mama says I do a very nice satin stitch."

A *kulig*, the cousins explained, was a night when the young people would dress in traditional peasant finery, wearing masks, and drive around the countryside in sleighs all night.

They brought along a band of hired musicians and a feast. At every manor house they carried in the feast and began dancing. "Usually the hosts only pretend to be surprised," giggled Antonia. "But sometimes they really don't know we're coming. We wake them up and make them dance!"

Dressed in her costume on the night of the *kulig*, Manya stared at herself in the mirror. She wore a full skirt, puffed out with several petticoats, a white blouse, a white lace-trimmed apron, and a black velvet vest. Ribbons trailed from her crown of blond braids. *I look like a different person*, thought Manya. She felt that she'd fallen into one of those novels she'd read at Zwola, in which young girls spent all their time getting dressed up and going to dances.

Where was Manya, the serious student with dark circles under her eyes, determined to win the gold medal if it killed her? That round-faced peasant girl in the mirror was free to dance and laugh, to have the time of her life. Manya and her cousins bundled up, jumped into the sleighs, and drove off with the horses' bells jingling. Young men, also in festive peasant costumes, escorted the sleighs on horseback. Their torches gleamed on the snow.

All night long, house after house, they danced the *mazurka* and *oberek*—Polish folk dances—and the waltz. Manya whirled from partner to partner with hardly a pause for breath. "You're the best dancer at the *kulig*," one boy whispered in her ear.

It was the middle of the next morning before the girls were home. Even then, Manya couldn't sleep. Slipping out of bed, she sat down at the desk to write to Kazia all about the magical night. Her pen raced across the page: "At eight o'clock in the morning we danced the last dance," she giddily reported.

★　★　★　★

The seasons changed, but Manya floated lazily through her year off with not a thought in her head. Soon enough she'd need to start working and worrying again. But in July 1884, when the enchanted year was supposed to end, a former student of Bronislava Sklodovska's invited Manya and Hela to her country estate for the rest of the summer. Their hostess was the Comtesse de Fleury.

"We are to take the train to the town nearest the estate," Hela announced, reading from the countess's telegraph, "where her coachman will pick us up in a carriage. Manya, a private carriage for us!"

The countess's château, Kepa, was set at the fork of two rivers northeast of Warsaw. The place was ideal for boating and swimming. Manya and Hela were given their own room with a view of the water and the woods.

The château was full of young guests like Manya and Hela, and the countess and her husband delighted in their high spirits. Manya was the ringleader in practical jokes. Her chief victim was one of the young men, the countess's brother Jan, who had a crush on her. Once, when Jan was away from the estate for a day, Manya and the other girls rearranged his room for him—by hanging all the furniture from the rafters.

Every evening at Kepa there was some kind of entertainment: games, dancing, parties. One night, in honor of their hosts' wedding anniversary, the young people presented them with a huge crown of vegetables. The youngest girl read out loud a poem composed by Manya. She demanded, in comic verse, that their hostess give a picnic and invite a boy for each of the girls.

"Indeed," retorted the countess, "I will do no such thing." The girls all groaned. Their hostess rose from her chair with a grand gesture. "No," she continued, "I will certainly not give you a picnic, you saucy girls!" She paused and smiled. "I will give you—a ball!" The girls, including Manya and Hela, broke into wild cheers.

Although Manya was delighted, she had to scramble for something to wear. "My dancing gown is so shabby, Hela! And I don't have any dancing slippers." But Manya had just enough money to buy cheap dancing shoes and a length of thin muslin to redrape the dress. At the ball, she danced every dance, and by morning she had actually danced through the soles of her slippers.

When the magical summer ended, Manya and Hela boarded the train to Warsaw. Their friends waved good-bye from the platform, and the Sklodovska girls waved back. Lancet poked his muzzle out the window beside them, barking and barking.

CHAPTER EIGHT

THE FLYING UNIVERSITY

In the autumn of 1884, Manya Sklodovska, plump and healthy after her year of happy idleness, was ready to get back to work. The family needed money, as always, so she would do her part to earn some. She was also eager to stretch the muscles of her mind again.

The Sklodovskis had moved again, back to Novolipki Street, not far from the boys' high school where Mr. Sklodovski used to be assistant director. This apartment was smaller than the one on Leszno Street, but at least there weren't any boarders. "Just our family—the old father and his three beautiful girls," said Vladislav Sklodovski. Jozio had received a scholarship, and he was studying medicine at the University of St. Petersburg in Russia.

Hela was taking voice lessons from one of Warsaw's finest teachers; if she didn't become an opera singer, she would probably become a teacher herself. Besides, there were several young men who wanted to marry Hela. Bronia was still keeping house for the family and giving private lessons in French and German. Sometimes Manya watched Bronia count her earnings, which she kept rolled in a stocking. The money added up very slowly. Manya helped Bronia with the housekeeping, and she began tutoring too.

One afternoon, as Manya was helping Bronia bundle washing for the laundress, Cousin Henrietta dropped by. Hearing Hela practicing her scales in the bedroom, Henrietta struck a pose like an opera singer and waggled her jaw up and down.

Bronia glanced up from the laundry. "What a clown you are, Henrietta. If you don't have anything better to do, you could tie up these parcels."

"Oh, but I do have something better to do," said Henrietta, suddenly serious. "Are you coming to"—she dropped her voice, although no one else was in the apartment—"Miss Piasecka's tonight?"

"The Flying University?" asked Bronia, also in a low voice. "Of course."

"Of course," Manya chimed in. She'd done the reading for the class, and she was looking forward to the lecture on positivism. "Why don't you stay for supper and go to the class with us?"

Henrietta agreed, but she could never stay serious for long. Before supper she'd talked Manya into cutting each other's hair—"to show how unconventional we are."

Glancing in the hall mirror just before they left, Manya wasn't sure that the haircut made her look unconventional. The short curls all over her head mainly made her face look rounder and plumper.

A little later, entering Miss Piasecka's drawing room with Bronia, Henrietta, and Bronia's friend Maria Rakowska, Manya felt the other young women staring at her cropped hair. She started to put her hand up to touch the short ends, but then forced it down to her side. She was glad when the lecture began and the students shifted their attention to the lecturer.

This speaker was one of the philosophers, called "positivists," who wanted Poland to solve its problems through thinking and working. Scientific progress and modern methods of farming and manufacturing were the key, he said, rather than armed rebellion. He explained how Polish society could progress if the peasants were educated in their own language.

"Polish society is still stuck in the Middle Ages," the lecturer declared. "The idle nobility want to keep their privileges. The peasants don't know enough to demand the rights they deserve. And so our nation stagnates."

The speaker went on to quote the words of a student leader at Warsaw University: "We have learned how to die intelligently, but never how to live intelligently."

The hair on the back of Manya's neck prickled. That was it, to live intelligently! There had already been too much noble fighting and dying. Poland would be redeemed through achievements in the sciences and industry, and through social reform. To take part in this work—*that* would be a truly noble life.

Manya knew that there were young people in Warsaw still plotting revolution. Socialist students, who believed that property like farms and factories should be held in common rather than privately owned, had organized a general strike two years ago. Many of them had been arrested and executed. Manya would never forget the grim night that she and Kazia had spent with their poor friend Leonie, keeping vigil for her condemned brother.

After the positivist finished his lecture, tea was served. The dozen women stood around Miss Piasecka's drawing room, sipping and talking excitedly. "Look at all the times Poles have tried to overthrow the Russian oppressors by armed rebellion," said Bronia. "The rebellion of 1831—a noble failure. The rebellion of 1863—another noble failure."

"And the results?" put in Miss Piasecka, a thin, intense woman. "Thousands of Poles killed. Thousands sent to Siberia in chain gangs."

"Yes, and thousands more forced to leave their homeland forever," said Jadwiga Sikorska, the headmistress of Manya's former school. Manya had heard that Miss Sikorska had also opened her home to the Flying University. The classes were often held in private homes, to keep them secret.

"And what was accomplished by the assassination of Tsar Alexander II?" asked Manya. "Nothing." She remembered how gleefully she and Kazia had danced when they had heard the news of his death. And how proud she had been when she'd learned that a Pole had killed him! But the next tsar, Alexander III, was ruling the Poles even more harshly than his father had.

The conversation turned to the emancipation of women. The main idea of the Flying University, of course, was that women had the same right to education as men. Manya's mother and father had always believed that, but she was excited now to realize how many others agreed with them.

"Have you read Eliza Orzeszkowa?" someone asked the group. "She's being punished for her stand on women's rights. The Russian police put her under surveillance, you know. She can't go for a walk in the park without being followed."

At the end of the evening Miss Piasecka announced, "My aunt's dressmaker is willing to let someone give classes to the women in her workshop. That is, she'll let us read aloud—of course the workers have to keep on sewing while they listen." She glanced around the circle.

"I'll do it," said Manya.

So every week Manya spent one morning at the dressmaker's workshop. She read to the seamstresses from the same books her father had read to his family, especially the great Polish poets. What she was doing was against the law, but it made her feel proud. If her teachers in the Flying University were risking imprisonment or exile for the sake of education, why shouldn't she?

While the workers cut and stitched and fitted, Manya read aloud. She noticed that many of the seamstresses were younger than she was. She at least had finished high school—some of these girls could barely read. "Thank you kindly, miss," they chorused when Manya finished.

Sometimes she wondered if the poetry of Adam Mickiewicz or Julian Niemcewicz meant anything to her students, but then a girl would lift her head from her work and give a sigh of satisfaction, and Manya knew these sessions were worthwhile. Manya brought the few books she could spare to the workshop and set up a small library for the seamstresses. She begged more books from her friends and relatives. This kind of teaching was certainly different from trying to pound French or mathematics into the heads of the privileged girls she tutored. Especially that one silly girl who fiddled with the ribbons on her braids the whole time!

In her spare time, Manya read to herself. She read positivists like Jozef Kraszewski, who believed in "slow and gradual progress through reforming individuals, increasing enlightenment, encouraging work, order, and moderation."

Manya read the Polish novelists Eliza Orzeszkowa and Boleslaw Prus, who were also positivists. She read biblical scholarship, Russian novels, French and German poetry. When she came across lines that particularly struck her, she copied them down. Sometimes she translated them into Polish. She also recorded her thoughts about what she read in her diary, as if she were having conversations with the authors. So many wonderful books, each one expanding the boundaries of her mind!

Every Saturday the Sklodovskis spent the evening, as they had for years, in private readings. Vladislav Sklodovski was a short, heavy man, always dressed in a conventional dark suit, with a quiet manner. But when he read aloud to his family, the passion and beauty of the words came through as powerfully as if he were a Greek god. Manya thought that if all Polish children could be taught the way her father had taught his own, Poland would indeed be transformed.

Manya herself was more determined than ever to become a teacher. But much as she loved poetry, it was physics that Manya wanted to teach. First she had to learn the subject herself. Not just from books, but in a laboratory with proper equipment.

CHAPTER NINE

MISS MARIA

One evening in the autumn of 1885, Manya came into Bronia's room while she was adding up her savings. Bronia had covered the back of an old envelope with arithmetic. It looked to Manya like the same addition and subtraction over and over, with the same discouraging result. "How much have you saved now?" she asked.

"Enough for third-class train fare to Paris and one year's rent." Bronia shook the old stocking where she kept her hoard, as if hoping for one more half ruble. She would need five years' rent to live and study in Paris while she earned her medical doctor's degree.

"At this rate," Manya told Bronia, "you'll

reach the Sorbonne at the tender age of fifty-three."

Bronia laughed. "That's ridiculous. I'm sure to get there by the age of . . . forty-seven." Bronia was trying to joke, but her last words came out in a bitter tone. She was already twenty, and many of her classmates were married.

Manya had been thinking about Bronia's plight for some time, and finally it was clear to her what had to be done. "Look," said Manya, sitting down on the edge of the bed so that Bronia's coins bounced, "I have a plan. I'm going to take a position as a full-time governess and make some decent money."

"A governess?" Bronia's eyes widened in horror. "No, Manya! That's a terrible idea. Governesses have a wretched life."

"As for you, Bronia," Manya went on, "you must go ahead and leave for Paris. I'll work and send you my salary until you get your medical degree."

"Oh, no, Manya!" repeated Bronia. "You can't do that. I've heard some stories. . . . A governess is expected to be a refined, educated lady, but then the family treats her like a scullery maid. I could never let you sacrifice yourself for my career."

"Who said I was going to sacrifice myself?" Manya answered. "Anyway, you're the one who's sacrificed for four years, keeping house and looking after Papa. Besides, I'm only going to work until you become a doctor. Then you can support me while *I* attend the Sorbonne."

"No, no. It's impossible for me to leave Papa now," said Bronia. "His health isn't good, and he'd be so lonely. . . . Hela can't be expected to look after him."

"Papa wants you to go," said Manya firmly. "I've talked to him. He'll be all right."

Bronia argued for a while, but finally Manya said, "Mama would want you to go to Paris."

Bronia looked shocked again. The girls

hardly ever talked about their mother; it was too sad, too painful. She was beyond their reach, in another world. It was almost as if Manya had said, in the same commanding tone, "Saint Mary would want you to go."

For a moment they stared at each other, and then Bronia bowed her head and nodded. She hugged Manya tight, whispering, "My dear little sister."

The next morning, Bronia began to pack. In October the whole family went to the train station to say good-bye to her. Bronia was traveling with her friend Maria Rakowska, who would also study at the Sorbonne.

And then Manya went to an employment agency to apply for a governess job. Fortunately her hair had grown out by now, so she looked like the conventional young woman people expected a governess to be. She was an adult now, with adult responsibilities and an adult name: Miss Maria Sklodovska.

* * * *

Miss Maria's first governess job was with a wealthy family in Warsaw, the Bielskis. She was expected to live in with her employers, but she had a little time off each day. She took the streetcar from the Bielskis' home to see her father.

Maria's first impression of the mother, Mrs. Bielski, was that she was sweet but rather ignorant. When she had guests for dinner or tea, Mrs. Bielski spoke French—but not very well. Maria even heard her make some mistakes in Polish grammar. Before long, Maria decided that Mrs. Bielski was not very sweet either. She ordered the housekeeper to tell Miss Sklodovska that she shouldn't use so much lamp oil in her bedroom. *Skimping on lamp oil for the governess!* thought Maria. *What stinginess, when they have plenty of money.* Mrs. Bielski had just treated herself to a complete new fall wardrobe.

At first the Bielski daughters, Ludvika

and Sonia, behaved fairly well for their new governess. Maria was dismayed that they were so far behind in their lessons, but she tried to be patient. On the third morning, though, eight-year-old Sonia wouldn't even try to work the arithmetic problems Maria wrote on her slate. Slumping in her chair, Sonia pushed out her lower lip. "I don't like arithmetic. It's too hard."

Ludvika, age eleven, laughed in a superior way. "It's too hard for *you*, that's for certain."

"Ludvika, please pay attention to your own lesson," said Maria sharply.

The older sister turned back to her lesson-book, but then she glanced slyly at the younger girl. She pushed out her lower lip like Sonia and whined, "Two times two is . . . I forget."

Before Maria could scold Ludvika, Sonia lunged at her sister and pinched her arm hard. Ludvika screeched.

"Mon Dieu!" exclaimed a voice from the

doorway, in a French accent so bad that Maria winced. "My goodness!" Mrs. Bielski, dressed to make morning calls on her friends, smiled as if Ludvika and Sonia were only puppies tussling with each other. "Mademoiselle Maria will have to keep better order in the classroom than this!"

Maria's heart sank. It was bad enough for Ludvika and Sonia to be quarrelsome, but how could their mother make light of it? She was deeply shocked.

Lessons were difficult, but Maria came to dread the family meals. Mrs. Bielski's husband, if he was home, would read the evening newspaper throughout the meal. Ludvika snickered when Sonia dripped soup on the tablecloth. Sonia tried to kick Ludvika under the table. No one even thought of discussing current events or sharing the interesting experiences of the day, as the Sklodovskis did.

Maria was too proud to complain about the

lamp oil, but she was not about to give up reading at night. She bought her own oil. Alone in her room, Maria escaped by writing letters to Kazia or to Bronia in Paris. She read poetry, scientific articles, French and German novels and plays. She couldn't help thinking that some of the wealthy social climbers in the novels she read were exactly like Mrs. Bielski and her family.

As autumn turned into winter, the cold and the dark made Maria's life harder and harder to bear. One evening she sat with Mrs. Bielski and the girls in the drawing room. Sonia was plowing her way through a piece at the piano while Mrs. Bielski and Ludvika exchanged smirks and rolled their eyes.

For a while Maria tried to ignore all three of them and read her book. But even with Maria's powers of concentration, it was hopeless. *"Excusé-moi, Madame Bielski,"* said Maria politely. "I am so tired tonight. I believe I will go to my room early."

"Mademoiselle Maria doesn't care for our company," said Ludvika. "She thinks she's too refined for us, although she wears hand-me-down dresses."

Maria felt a surge of anger and disgust, but she kept her face a polite blank. She rose and left the room without answering. To her surprise, Mrs. Bielski followed her to the staircase. "Is that the trouble, Mademoiselle Maria?" she asked sharply. "Do you regard us as below you, although we pay your salary?"

Pausing with her hand on the railing, Maria turned to answer. In fact, since Maria stood on the staircase, her employer *was* literally below her. Maria was reminded of Miss Mayer at the government high school, who had been so angry that Maria was taller.

"Madame Bielski, to tell you the truth, it is unpleasant for me to live and work in a household where I am neither liked nor respected. But it is quite unbearable to live with a family whose members treat *each other* with spite and disrespect."

Even in the lamplight, Mrs. Bielski's face looked red. "Mademoiselle," she said in her atrocious French accent, "your services are no longer required. And don't expect me to write you a letter of recommendation."

"Madame," answered Maria, "a letter of recommendation from this household would be of no use to me." She sprang up the stairs to her room, feeling enormously relieved.

But as Maria began to pack her few belongings, she burst into tears. "Oh, Bronia!" she pleaded, thinking of her promise to her sister. "I'm so sorry! I just couldn't bear this hell one moment longer."

The next day Maria calmed down and talked it over with her father. She realized that quitting had probably been the sensible thing to do, anyway. She hadn't saved much money. She'd had to pay for streetcar fare every day when she went home to visit her father, and the cost of lamp oil had added up. Besides, her life as a governess was so dreary that she often stopped in shops and bought little treats to cheer herself: a pastry, a ribbon, a used book.

Back home for Christmas, Maria thought about what to do next. She might find a governess job with a more pleasant family in Warsaw. But there would still be the expenses of the streetcar every day. And as long as Maria lived in the city, she'd be tempted by all the nice things to buy.

At the employment agency, Maria heard about a family in the country who was looking for a governess. They offered a good salary: five hundred rubles a year. If she lived on a country estate, there would be nothing to buy. And Maria loved the country! She thought fondly of the plane tree house and the gooseberries of Zwola, and of the gardens and rivers on the Comtesse de Fleury's estate.

On the other hand, if she ended up in another bad situation, signing the contract for this position would be like condemning herself to exile for the next three years. But if Uncle Henryk had endured four years in Siberia for the sake of Poland, couldn't Maria stand three years in the country for Bronia's sake?

On January 1, 1886, Maria Sklodovska set out for Szczuki, a village sixty miles north of Warsaw. The train pulled out of the Warsaw station well before dawn. Feeling heavy with sadness, Maria sat down in the third-class railway car. During the brief hours of daylight, she watched the Polish plains through the frost patterns on the window. The train chugged past villages of log houses with thatched roofs—peasants' huts. It passed through towns with church spires; once in a while, she glimpsed a castle in the distance.

Before leaving Warsaw, Maria had been too

busy to think much about the next three years. But now she was filled with anxiety. She had left all her family and friends behind. She was going to live with strangers.

Maria only knew a little about the Zorawskis. They weren't landowners; they managed a plantation for a Polish sugar-beet magnate. They had seven children, but she wasn't expected to teach them all. The youngest boy and girl weren't old enough for lessons. The three other sons were away, the oldest at Warsaw University, and the two younger ones at boarding school.

Maria had been hired to teach the two older daughters. One was ten years old. The other was the same age as Maria, which might make teaching difficult. Of course Maria, a star student from Warsaw, was much more advanced in her studies than the Zorawskis' daughter, but that didn't mean the girl would respect her.

The employment agency had told Maria that the Zorawskis had been "dissatisfied" with their last governess. Maybe they'd be dissatisfied with her, too. What if the Zorawskis were just as awful as the Bielski family? How could she stand three years in Szczuki, when she couldn't stand even three months with the Bielskis?

After hours on the train, Maria climbed down from the cold railway car to the even icier platform of a little country railway depot. One or two gas lamps dimly lit sleighs waiting for the few passengers. Her journey was only half over.

Bundled into a horse-drawn sleigh, Maria rode on and on through the dark, frozen countryside. The squeak of the sleigh runners and the jingle of the harness bells sounded loudly in the snow-muffled silence. From her burrow of wraps, she could see only bare-branched trees and the snow-covered fields beyond. It seemed like she was traveling the same stretch of straight road over and over endlessly.

When the sleigh finally pulled up in front of the Zorawski manor house, it was the middle of the night, but the family turned out to welcome her. Mr. and Mrs. Zorawski invited her inside and introduced their older daughter, Bronka; their ten-year-old girl, Andzia; and their littlest boy, Stas. "You must be exhausted, my dear Miss Maria," said Mrs. Zorawska. "Come into the parlor for some hot tea. Then I'll show you your room."

They actually seemed glad to see her, thought Maria. Maybe it wouldn't be so dreadful here after all.

CHAPTER TEN

EXILE AND FIRST LOVE

In the light of the next day, Maria saw that Szczuki was hardly a country paradise—nothing like Zwola or Kempa. Her room on the second floor of the manor house was large and comfortably furnished, and well heated with a beehive-shaped porcelain stove. But outside her window loomed an enormous redbrick chimney, blocking part of the sky and smudging the rest of it with smoke. It was the smokestack of the sugar-beet refinery. Instead of the woods and meadows Maria had imagined, flat acres of sugar-beet fields stretched out to the horizon.

Never mind! Beautiful scenery would have been nice, but it was much more important that Maria's employers, the Zorawskis, seemed so agreeable. Maria made friends immediately with the older girl, Bronka. Teaching Bronka turned out to be more like helping a sister with her homework, very friendly and natural.

Mr. Zorawski seemed intelligent, in a down-to-earth way, and proud of his management of the sugar-beet plantation. The first day he gave Maria a tour of the estate. "I may say," he remarked as he handed her into the buggy, "that Szczuki has become something of a model for the industry. Sugar-beet farmers from all over Europe visit us to see how we apply the most advanced and scientific techniques."

"I'd like to observe your techniques during the growing season," said Maria. "And will you show me the factory? I'm so interested in the process of refining beet sugar."

"Indeed!" Mr. Zorawski gave her a surprised but pleased look. Halting the buggy in front of the factory, he took her in and led her among the vats and machinery. He introduced her to the engineers and technicians. Maria asked many questions, especially of the chemist.

Back in the buggy an hour later, Mr. Zorawski turned to Maria with a twinkle in his eye. "If I may say so, Miss Sklodovska, of all the many pleasant young ladies I've met, you're the first who ever seemed interested in the sugar-beet industry—other than how much money her papa could make from it to buy her ball gowns!"

Maria met his gaze seriously. "I've always spent summers on farms and helped with the farmwork, so I suppose I naturally think growing crops is interesting. And I hope to study science and become a science teacher one day. I believe I can help our people better themselves that way. Knowledge ought to be used for the benefit of the people, don't you think?"

"I do, indeed," he answered quietly. As they continued the tour of the estate, he explained this and that to her as he would to another businessman, without talking down. At the end of the tour he said, "Miss Sklodovska, I have a number of scientific books in my library. You're welcome to borrow them anytime you like."

"Thank you so much!" she answered. Ball gowns were very nice, but science books—now, that was a real joy.

Mrs. Zorawska was a little more difficult than her husband. Maria found that out when her lady employer began planning the first winter ball. Mrs. Zorawska gave Maria an invitation list and a stack of fine notepaper for writing the invitations. Maria nodded and put the paper aside, intending to get to it after she answered her letters from home.

The next day Mrs. Zorawska popped into the classroom to ask for the invitations. "I haven't had time to write them yet," said Maria. "I'll—"

"What!" Mrs. Zorawska scowled, and she actually stamped her foot. "I thought I made it clear that they had to go out *at once*."

Maria must have looked shocked. After Mrs. Zorawska had swept out of the classroom, Bronka whispered, "Don't mind Mama, Miss Maria. She only flies into a temper because she's anxious for the ball to go well. She doesn't mean anything by it."

Sure enough, when Maria handed her a stack of neatly written invitations that evening, Mrs. Zorawska beamed at her. "Dear Miss Maria! What elegant handwriting you have. Now, I want you to enjoy our ball as much as anyone. Bronka has a blue gown that would look very becoming on you, don't you, Bronka?"

The night of the ball, Bronka's maid helped Maria into Bronka's blue silk gown. "Look how that color sets off your ash-blond hair and gray eyes!" exclaimed Bronka. "You'll be the belle of the ball, Miss Maria."

Holding up their trains, Bronka and Maria rustled down the front stairs. In the ballroom, the merry music of the violins and the light from the chandeliers, reflecting off the polished floor, lifted Maria's spirits. Maybe tonight she could forget she was a governess and just have a good time.

Maria's dance card filled up quickly. As long as she was whirling around to the strains of a polka, *mazurka*, or a waltz, she enjoyed herself. But between dances, as she tried to talk to the guests, she felt more and more out of place.

During the buffet supper, Maria whispered to Bronka, "These girls dance very well, but do they ever do *anything* besides attend parties and gossip? I can't imagine them discussing positivism or higher education for women—if they've even heard of such things."

"There truly are *some* intelligent girls in the neighborhood," said Bronka apologetically, "but they couldn't come to our ball tonight."

Maria excused herself before the last dance. Upstairs, she sat down to report to Kazia before she went to bed. "The young people here are most uninteresting," she wrote. "Some of the girls are so many geese who never open their mouths, the others are highly provocative."

As the weeks of winter went by, Maria missed Warsaw, with its buzz of discussion about positivism and women's rights. She missed her family. She wrote long letters to Bronia in Paris; to Cousin Henrietta, now married and living in Lvov, in the Austrian-ruled section of Poland; to her brother Jozef; and to her father. Her father, in great excitement, wrote Maria that a German chemist had discovered a new element, which he named *germanium*. Mendeleev, with his periodic table of the elements, had predicted that an element with the properties of germanium had to exist.

Despite feeling homesick, Maria tried to be grateful for the pleasant moments she enjoyed in Szczuki. After the hours for lessons, Maria and Bronka skated on the frozen ponds. There were some jolly sleigh rides. The river could be lovely—at least, upstream from the sugar-beet refinery. Downstream, it was choked with industrial sludge.

After the sugar beets were planted in the spring, Maria sometimes walked out to the fields with Mr. Zorawski to see how the crops were coming along. On the muddy road through the village, they often met the peasants who lived in the huts near the refinery. She knew that the local gentry who came to the Zorawskis' parties looked down on these people who worked with their hands. Those who labored, in their eyes, were inferior to those who didn't work at all. Maria wondered what they'd think of her mother, who had made shoes for all the Sklodovski children.

Maria made regular trips to the stables to visit the horses, treating them to sugar lumps and rubbing their noses. The draft horses made Maria think of the peasants on the road, the way they plodded with their heads down. Her heart ached for the peasants, especially the children. Would they find a way to learn and better themselves? Or would they simply grow up and keep on plodding, the way their parents had?

During the spring thaw, Maria knocked on the door of Mr. Zorawski's office. "Sir, I have a favor to ask," she said. "Would you allow me to give classes to the peasants' children in my spare time?"

Mr. Zorawski looked at her over his reading spectacles. "Classes to the peasants?" he repeated in surprise.

"It seems such a shame for them to grow up ignorant," Maria explained. "And a shame for our society too. You see, I truly believe that Poland would be a nobler—and more successful—land if education were open to everyone."

Maria twisted her hands nervously as she spoke. She was asking for permission to do something illegal. The Russians rulers didn't want the peasants educated, and they certainly didn't want them educated in Polish. Maria added, "These ideas are a tradition in my family. My grandfather Sklodovski, the headmaster of a school, insisted that peasant children be allowed to study there."

To Maria's relief, Mr. Zorawski nodded thoughtfully. "I don't see why not," he said. "I admire your idealism, Miss Maria."

Bronka admired Maria even more than her father did. When Maria asked her to help with the new project, she immediately agreed. Maria warned her, "You know if we are reported to the police, we'll be sent to Siberia."

Bronka nodded, her eyes shining. She eagerly began to gather schoolroom equipment and to spread the news about the class to the peasant families. Maria herself was excited, dreaming of introducing the peasant children to Polish history and literature.

On the first day of class, ten barefoot, ragged peasant children climbed the outside staircase to Maria's room. Maria and Bronka had carried in a table and chairs, and Maria had bought notebooks and pens for her pupils with her own money.

After the first class, Maria and Bronka exchanged dismayed glances. "Oh, dear," they said at the same time.

"They don't even know the alphabet," groaned Maria. "Or if they do, they only know the Russian letters."

"And they don't have any idea how to behave in school!" said Bronka. "They sniffled and snorted the whole time they were trying to copy the letters. And with ten of them all together in this warm room—well, they *smelled*. I wish we could scrub them outside the door."

"I don't suppose they have hot water in their huts," said Maria with a sigh. She put aside her ideas about teaching literature and history. It would be an accomplishment just to teach the peasant children to read and write.

As the classes went on, some of the pupils did make progress. Tears came to Maria's eyes, watching a child finally make sense of the black marks on white paper. It wasn't fair that learning was so hard for these children and so easy for her.

By the beginning of the summer, the grass in the manor gardens was soft green, and bees hummed in the flower beds. "Didn't I tell you the garden would be pretty when summer came?" Bronka asked Maria. "I love summer! Mama just asked the gardener to set up the croquet ground. And tomorrow Casimir comes home from Warsaw! Oh, I know you'll like him, Maria. He's the nicest, sweetest brother."

Maria did like the Zorawskis' oldest son right away. Casimir had a dashing blond mustache and an open smile. He talked amusingly about life at the university, where he was studying mathematics. But he also listened to Maria with sincere attention.

"Does it seem dull in the country, Miss Maria, compared with your life in Warsaw?" asked Casimir. The young people were playing croquet on the grass under the ash trees. He swung his croquet mallet, and his yellow ball rolled through a hoop and knocked hers.

"I do miss the discussions about politics and social issues," said Maria. "Your sister Bronka is a dear, and she says there are intelligent girls, besides her, in the neighborhood. But I can't say much for the ones I've met."

"What about the young men?" Casimir asked. He kept his eyes on his ball, but Maria thought they twinkled. His next swing was a bit off, and his ball hit the side of the wicket and rolled back. "Rats! Are you trying to distract me, Miss Maria?"

"Not a bit," she replied. She didn't answer his first question. With a steady swing she hit her ball so that it glanced off his and rolled through the wicket. She looked at Casimir to see if he minded being beaten at croquet. Many young men, especially the ones who lived around Szczuki, would. But Casimir let out a good-natured laugh.

"As for me," he said, "I've never been happier to be home for the summer."

He really was the nicest, the most charming young man she had ever met, Maria decided. She felt a bit light-headed. It was probably because of these long midsummer days, when eight o'clock in the evening seemed like the middle of the afternoon.

Summer passed quickly, Casimir returned to Warsaw, and life at Szczuki settled into humdrum stretches. Maria wished so much that ten-year-old Andzia were more like her older sister. Andzia had trouble concentrating on lessons for more than ten minutes at a time. When Maria was in the middle of giving her a French dictation or explaining an arithmetic problem, Andzia might hear a friend of her mother's arriving downstairs. Then she'd jump up unthinkingly and run to the head of the stairs to look.

Andzia's lessons were supposed to begin promptly at eight o'clock, but she liked to stay up late and sleep late. Sometimes Maria would go looking for her pupil at eight fifteen and find her still burrowed under the down comforter. Those mornings, she had to drag Andzia out of bed.

Maria tried not to get frustrated, but she couldn't help it. What was the matter with this girl? At home in the Sklodovski household, everyone was out of bed before the clock had finished striking six. Even Hela, who wasn't as scholarly as the rest of the family, would never dare to oversleep on a school day.

On Maria's nineteenth birthday, November 7, 1886, she started the day feeling rather sorry for herself. She did notice that Andzia seemed to be trying harder with her lessons than usual, though, and that Bronka had a mysterious smile. Then, at dinner, Mrs. Zorawska herself carried in a special cake with pink sugar icing. Andzia marched behind her mother with a bouquet of hothouse flowers, which she presented to Maria. "Happy birthday, dear Maria!" crowed Bronka. They all sang to her and clapped. Mr. Zowarski, with a bow, handed her a book—a treatise on modern agriculture.

"How kind you all are to me!" exclaimed Maria. She felt ashamed of being discontented. The Zorawskis had really taken her in as a member of the family, it seemed. She silently vowed that she would have a better attitude from now on.

During her free time, Maria tried to keep up her own studies. She borrowed chemistry and physics books from the refinery office and puzzled over them as best she could by herself. She studied mathematics, too, with her father's help—he often included problems for her to solve in his letters.

Then Casimir came back to Szczuki for the Christmas holidays. Maria was in the stable, treating the horses to sugar lumps, when he arrived. She heard him greeting the stable hands, and his booted footsteps on the stable floor. "Miss Maria," he said. She turned to see him looking at her with eager, soft eyes.

Maria felt shaky inside. "Mr. Casimir. I didn't know you were home yet." She thought her own eyes must be eager and soft, and to hide them she turned back to her favorite horse, a bay mare. She kissed the mare on the nose. Then she felt more confused than before. She looked over her shoulder at

Casimir, and they both burst out laughing.

Casimir and Maria were often together that season. It wouldn't have been proper for them to be alone, but during the sleigh rides and other gatherings they always somehow ended up side by side. They had so much to talk about.

"I'll probably join Father in managing the sugar-beet business here," Casimir told her one afternoon as they skated over the frozen river. "I hope I'll be respected and admired the way he is."

"I do respect your father," said Maria, "but don't you think that more should be done to improve the lot of the peasants? I think you could make a big difference in their lives."

"I'd be proud if I could make such a difference," he answered. "Would you be proud of me then?"

"Of course," said Maria. "I'm always proud of my friends when they do well." She knew he was asking something more than that, but she felt shy. She added, "I hope so much to make a contribution to society myself. That's why I want to teach science." Casimir listened seriously, nodding.

One afternoon the young people of the neighborhood gathered at Szczuki. The weather was cold but clear, and they went outside to build a snow fort. They teased and threw snowballs as they worked, but before long they had a fort with thick walls higher than their heads.

"The architects in Warsaw would be impressed!" said Casimir. "See here: doors, windows—even a tower, with steps leading up!"

"I'm impressed," laughed his sister Bronka, "but listen, there's the bell ringing at the house. It's time for tea, and I'm starved!" The others ran back toward the manor house, and Maria started to follow.

"Please stay a moment, Miss Maria," called Casimir from the tower. "Come see how the sunset colors the snow."

Maria climbed the snow steps, taking Casimir's hand as he reached down to help her. At the top, instead of letting go, he wrapped both hands around hers. She looked west, at the rose-colored fields. "It's beautiful," she said breathlessly. "But please let go."

Casimir slowly let her hand slide out of his. "I don't ever want to let you go," he said. "I've never known a girl like you, Miss Maria. You're so intelligent, so good, so fine, and"—his voice sank lower—"you're beautiful." He clasped her hand again, and this time she let him keep it.

Maria and Casimir talked in soft murmurs as the light faded. Before it was completely dark, they had pledged to spend the rest of their lives together. Crossing the snowy lawn with her hand tucked into Casimir's arm, Maria felt that the sunset still glowed around them.

"I wish you didn't have to leave for Warsaw tomorrow," she said.

"If only I didn't have to go back so soon!" Casimir exclaimed. "You'll write me every day, won't you? At least I can talk to Father and Mother about us this evening. Then in Warsaw I'll call on your father."

Maria nodded, imagining their love as an avenue of light and warmth stretching from Szczuki to Warsaw. The proper way to go about an engagement was to consult the parents first, before anyone else knew. She was sure that her father would welcome Casimir as a son-in-law—how could anyone dislike Casimir?

After dinner, Maria sat down on a sofa in the sewing room. Casimir was in the parlor with his mother and father. In a short while, she expected, the Zorawskis would rush out of the parlor, beaming at her as they had on her birthday.

Maria finished the lace collar she was crocheting for Bronka and glanced at the clock on the mantel. Casimir and his parents had been in there since half past eight. What was taking so long?

The parlor was down the hall from the sewing room, and at first Maria couldn't hear any voices. Then she detected Mr. Zorawski's deep tones, barking out questions. Mrs. Zorawska joined in, her voice shrill and rising. What could be wrong?

At a quarter past nine Maria heard the parlor door open and close, and Casimir came down the hall. She recognized his footsteps, although they were slower than usual. As he entered the sewing room, he was biting his lip. "What's the matter?" she asked, rising.

Casimir stopped just inside the doorway, looking at the floor. He said, "I think it's best for us to wait. Father was quite upset. So was Mother, for that matter. She almost fainted."

"I don't understand," said Maria slowly. Her face was burning as if Casimir had slapped her. "Why should they be upset?"

"Well, you see—I thought they'd already guessed—I thought they must have noticed—but it seems it had never entered their minds that you and I might—"

"They don't think it's a suitable match," said Maria quietly. Her heart felt pierced, and it was hard to breathe.

"Well, I think it may take a while for them to get used to the idea." Casimir gave her a pleading look. "I tried to explain how much I loved you, that there was no other girl like you, and never would be. . . ."

"They want you to marry a girl with money," Maria went on. Every word was painful, but she forced herself to say it. "They don't want you to marry a governess."

Nodding, he bit his lip again.

CHAPTER ELEVEN

MARIA ENTERS THE LABORATORY

If it hadn't been for her promise to Bronia, Maria would have left Szczuki the next day. It was bad enough that Mr. and Mrs. Zorawska considered her unworthy of their son. But that her beloved Casimir wouldn't stand up to them, *that* was the dagger in her heart. He was miserable, but he would not tell his parents that they were wrong. How could he be so weak, if he truly loved her? How could she love him, if he was so weak?

In her humiliation Maria remembered a short story by Eliza Orzeszkowa, one of her favorite Polish authors. "Miss Antonina" was a story about a young governess in a landowner's family. Antonina falls in love, but the romance is blighted. She spends her whole life as a governess and finally dies alone, old and poor, still treasuring a picture of the young man.

So this was romantic love, Maria told herself in a silent fury. In her opinion, falling in love was like catching a bad cold: very unpleasant, likely to happen, and it might take a while to get over it. That didn't mean that Maria Sklodovska had to give in to it, like pathetic Miss Antonina or the empty-headed girls of Szczuki society. Bronislava and Vladislav Sklodovski had brought up their daughter to have more strength of character than that!

Maria, by sheer willpower, would focus on her goal. She would stay at this well-paying job and support Bronia through her medical studies. In the meantime, she'd prepare herself for her own turn at the Sorbonne. She'd continue to study mathematics, with her father's long-distance help. She'd learn chemistry as best she could, without a laboratory.

Maria would also continue her classes for the Polish peasant children. There were eighteen of them coming to her room twice a week now. If these people who lived close to the land could be given their rightful inheritance, Polish history and literature, the nation of Poland might come into her true glory. *That* was much more important than the blighted romance of Maria Salome Sklodovska.

Somehow the three years in Szczuki dragged by. In October 1888, Maria received a letter from her friend Kazia. The letter bubbled over with good news: Kazia was engaged, and supremely happy. Not only that, thought Maria indignantly, but Kazia's fiancé was a German! How could she consider marrying anyone but a Pole?

Maria wasn't in a mood to be understanding, because she'd just been through a week of torment. Casimir had come home for a few days, and he'd followed Maria around the house with longing looks and soft whispers. Mr. and Mrs. Zorawski watched them, unsmiling. Maria couldn't help feeling pulled toward Casimir again, even though she told herself it was hopeless.

In November of 1888, there was no cake, and there were no flowers, to celebrate Miss Maria's birthday. Bronka wished her many happy returns when they were alone together, but otherwise no one said a word. Of course there was nothing from Casimir at Warsaw University! *He wouldn't dare write a letter that his parents might see,* thought Maria furiously.

Alone in her room that night, Maria put her head down on her dressing table and began to cry, making noises like a wounded animal. Then she jerked up her head, as if someone else were pulling her by the hair, and stared in the mirror. Her trembling lips tightened, and her chin pushed out. "This will never do," she said sharply. She got up and splashed cold water on her face.

Maria Salome Sklodovska would not let herself be beaten down by the Zorawskis, by the dreariness of life among the sugar-beet fields, or by Imperial Russia and their stupid rules against higher education for women. The prison term of her years at Szczuki would be over next spring. Meanwhile, Maria would endure.

A few days before Easter 1889, Maria's train pulled into the Warsaw station. She took a deep breath of the smoky city air and thought, *Now I'll start feeling like myself again.* In Warsaw she'd be surrounded by intelligent, ambitious people, thinking, planning, and studying. The Flying University would be open to her once more, and she couldn't wait to sign up.

At home, the Sklodovski family wasn't as pinched for money as before. For the last two years, Vladislav Sklodovski had worked as the director of a reform school near Warsaw. Now

Mr. Sklodovski was retired for good.

"Dear little Manya!" he said as they sat by the samovar on her first evening back in Warsaw. "I'm so grateful to have you home, especially with Hela working in the provinces. Jozef's thinking of taking a position as a country doctor too."

"Yes, I know," said Maria. Her chin jutted out with determination. "We *must* get him a grant so he can afford to stay in Warsaw and study. And I'm sure I can find Hela a teaching job in Warsaw, even if I have to beg our important friends on my knees!" She added in a low voice, "Being stuck in the country is like . . . living in a hole in the ground." Her father, back to reading his scientific journal, didn't hear.

In Paris, Bronia had gotten engaged just before Maria returned to Warsaw. Her fiancé was another Polish medical student, Casimir Dluski. He was a fiery Socialist, wanted by the

Russians for subversive activities in Warsaw. That meant that Bronia couldn't bring him home, and so the wedding would have to take place in Paris.

Almost before Maria had settled back into her life in Warsaw, a letter from Bronia arrived. Recognizing her sister's handwriting, Maria expected the letter to be full of more news about the wedding. Sure enough, Bronia went on about how wonderful Casimir Dluski was. Why, Maria thought, wincing, did Bronia's fiancé have to have the same first name as Casimir Zorawski?

But the second page of Bronia's letter made Maria's eyes open wide. "And now you, my little Manya: You must make something of your life sometime. If you can get together a few hundred rubles this year, you can come to Paris next year and live with us." Bronia calculated that Maria would only need enough money for train fare to Paris and her student fees at the Sorbonne if she lived with her sister and brother-in-law.

Paris, next year! Maria stared at the letter as if it were a ticket to paradise. Only . . . how could she leave Papa? He'd worked so hard, for so long, and his life had been so sad. He'd given everything for his children.

"Did the post come, Manya?" Vladislav Sklodovski called from the study.

"Yes, a letter from Bronia." Maria carried it into the study. "I'll read it to you." She read out loud the first part, about the wedding plans, and then skipped to the very end, Bronia's kisses and hugs for both of them. Best not to upset Papa, because Maria knew she couldn't bring herself to leave him.

But—was she going to give up her chance for a university education? Were her talents (surely she did have *some* talents) and hard work going to go to waste?

At least Maria could keep on studying,

through the Flying University. The first lecture she attended was by Cousin Jozef Boguski, about his work in Saint Petersburg as assistant to the great chemist Mendeleev.

After the lecture Maria told Cousin Jozef about her struggle to learn chemistry at Szczuki without a laboratory. "Come to the Museum of Industry and Agriculture," Jozef urged her. "I think you'll be pleased with our exhibits on sugar-beet farming," he said with a wink.

The Museum of Industry and Agriculture, a private institution in Warsaw, really did feature beet farming in one of its exhibits, but the building also held a laboratory, and as director of the Museum, Jozef could grant his cousin access. With great excitement, Maria took her chemistry and physics books to the museum and set up the experiments they described.

"Physics apparatus," Maria whispered to herself, remembering the fascinating instruments in her father's glass cabinet. Maria was twenty-one now, and science was more fascinating to her than ever. Finally, it was as if the glass cabinet were unlocked and Manya was allowed to play with the bright, beautiful objects.

Maria soon found that actual experiments in an actual laboratory didn't always turn out the way they did in the books. Sometimes the experiments failed completely, and Maria plunged into despair. Sometimes they worked better than she expected, and her spirits soared. But overall, she was simply happy. These were real experiments! The word "experiment," after all, meant that you couldn't be sure what was going to happen until you tried it.

When Cousin Jozef had time, he gave Maria advice about how to use the equipment or different procedures to try. He also introduced her to another chemist, a man who had studied with the great Robert Bunsen in Germany. "It's so kind of you to help me," she told them. "I can't thank you enough."

"It's only right," said Cousin Jozef with a shrug. "If Professor Mendeleev, creator of the periodic table of the elements, could take time to teach me, why shouldn't I teach you?"

"And Mendeleev himself learned from Professor Bunsen," added the other chemist. "That's how science progresses."

Maria would have liked to spend all her waking hours in the laboratory, but she could spare only Saturdays and Sundays. She'd taken a new job as a governess with a family in Warsaw. Fortunately, this job was turning out much better than the ones she'd had with the Bielskis or the Zorawskis.

Maria was satisfied with the way family affairs were turning out too. She'd managed to find Hela a decent teaching job and bring her back to the city. Their brother, Jozef, did receive a grant to stay in Warsaw, and Maria helped him with plans for *his* wedding.

Meanwhile, Maria began receiving pleading letters from Casimir Zorawski. He still loved her, he said. He begged for one last meeting, at least. Was it possible, she wondered, that Casimir would defy his parents and marry a girl without money?

At the end of the summer of 1891, over breakfast one morning, Maria said, "Papa, I've been thinking how nice it would be to take a vacation in the Tatra Mountains. You know, some of our friends are going, and September is a beautiful time of year."

"What a splendid idea!" Mr. Sklodovski beamed at his daughter over the butter dish. "You've been working too hard, my dear, between your teaching and your studies. You haven't had a real vacation for years." A twinkle came into his eye. "Besides . . . am I right in thinking that a certain young man might turn up in the mountains too?"

Maria blushed. It was impossible to have any secrets in this family! Hela must have said something, and Papa must have seen the return address on Casimir's letters. "I'll tell you all about it, Papa," she said, "but not until afterward." She'd agreed to one more meeting with Casimir.

When Maria arrived at the mountain resort, there was a note waiting for her. Casimir was staying at a nearby inn, and he asked her to meet him for a walk.

At the sight of his face, with his tender smile beneath his blond mustache, Maria's heart leaped. Casimir kissed her hand. "Maria! It's been such a long time. I've missed you so much."

Maria's heart was beating fiercely, but she said only, "Let's take the path through the high valley, shall we?"

While they walked through pinewoods and crossed rushing streams, Casimir chatted as if they'd just seen each other last week. He talked about his travels to places that Maria would find fascinating, and a book he'd read that reminded him of her, and a new horse of his that Maria would surely like. At first Maria kept up her part of the conversation. But the more they talked, the more uncomfortable she felt. Finally she interrupted him. "You didn't talk to your parents after all, did you?"

"Of course I did!" he said indignantly. "I promised I would, didn't I?"

"But you didn't tell them what *you'd* decided," said Maria. She seemed to see Casimir's handsome face at a distance now, and he looked young and weak to her. "You still think you have to let your parents decide what's right for you. Your parents, who would be glad if you married an idle society woman! As for me, I don't admire your parents' values. And I don't admire you for giving in to them."

"But can't you see it from their point of

view?" Casimir pleaded. "My father and mother want me to be well settled. They have nothing against you personally, but . . . Maria, I beg you, don't be angry with me."

Maria stopped on the path and fixed him with her clear gray eyes. "*My* parents, if they knew you, would have nothing against *you* personally. But they would tell me, Maria, self-sacrifice for a noble cause is glorious. Self-sacrifice for an unworthy person, on the other hand, is a waste and a sin."

"Maria—"

"Good-bye, Mr. Zorawski." Turning, Maria walked back to the resort by herself.

Back home in Warsaw, Maria scribbled a letter to Bronia in Paris. "I can come now." There was just enough time for her to make all the arrangements, pack, and arrive in time to register for classes at the Sorbonne.

CHAPTER TWELVE

PARIS AT LAST

One morning early in November 1891, Maria Sklodovska climbed into a third-class railway car in the Warsaw station. She was almost twenty-four, but at last she was on her way to Paris.

Her brother Jozef followed carrying a cluster of bags and parcels tied with string: books, food, and drink for three days. He also had a folding chair tucked under one arm. Maria would need the chair during the leg of the trip through Germany, where she could save money by riding fourth class. The fourth-class cars were cheap because they had only a few benches; they were almost like freight cars.

Maria set down a folded quilt to reserve

her seat by a window, while Jozef lofted her provisions for the journey into an overhead net. Then they hurried back out of the train to Mr. Sklodovski and Helena waiting on the platform.

At the sight of her father leaning on his walking stick, Maria's throat hurt and her eyes smarted. He had turned into a little old man. How could she leave him again? "As soon as I've finished my studies," she promised, kissing him, "I'll be back."

Vladislav Sklodovski hugged his youngest daughter. "Come back quickly, my dear little Manya. Work hard. Good luck!"

The train whistle sounded. Hela pressed a paper bag of caramels into her hand, and Maria ran up the steps. The puffing steam engine began to pull the train out of the station. Maria waved from the window. "Good-bye, Papa! Good-bye, Hela! Good-bye, Jozio!"

Maria could hardly believe she was actually

setting off on the adventure she'd dreamed of for so long. This journey seemed like part of the "Geography" game she and her brother and sisters used to play with colored blocks. She remembered Jozio telling her, "It's farther from Poland to France than it is from Poland to Austria."

Traveling to her governess's job in Szczuki almost six years ago, Maria had felt that she was going into exile. Now she was really leaving her native land, but she was traveling in triumph. All those years of hard work, sacrifice, and anxious planning were paying off, and she was on her way to one of the best universities in the world. She was doing it all for Poland, so that she could return and pass on the precious gifts of her education to her people.

The train ride from Warsaw to Paris would take forty hours. First, the tracks led westward toward the border between the Russian Empire and the German Empire. Maria was exhausted from the weeks of frantic preparations, but she couldn't relax until the train had passed the first border in the middle of the night. She checked her satchel a dozen times to make sure her traveling documents were still there. Maria's papers were in order, but what if the Russian border guards detained her on a whim?

All the next day the train chugged its way westward across northern Germany, through Berlin. Maria dozed in her folding chair, wearing her long coat and swaddled in the quilt, since there was no heat in the fourth-class car. It seemed like a dream when they reached the French border that night. Guards entered the car, carrying lanterns, to check the passengers' papers again.

And the next morning, like a dream come true, the train pulled into the last stop of Maria's thousand-mile journey, under the vaulted glass roof of the Gare du Nord. She felt queasy from the long jolting, swaying ride, and she had a crick in her neck from sleeping in her chair, but at last she had arrived in Paris.

"Maria!" She looked up and saw a young man waving at her as she climbed down the steps. It was her brother-in-law, Casimir Dluski. He seized her hands and kissed her on both cheeks. "I knew you at once—you look like my darling Bronia, only more stubborn. How was your journey? Come, let's claim your baggage."

"It's a wooden trunk, labeled "'M.S.,'" said Maria. All her worldly possessions, except for the mattress she'd sent ahead by freight, were in that trunk.

The Dluskis' apartment was near the train station, in a working-class neighborhood of Paris. To register at the Sorbonne a few days later, Maria had to take a horse-drawn bus to the Gare de l'Est, and then another bus across the city to the university. Maria rode in the cheapest bus seats, of course, climbing a cork-screw iron staircase to the open second deck.

It was chilly on top of the bus in November, but at least Maria had a good view of the city. The bus lurched and crawled along through miles of streets, first rolling past small ordinary apartment buildings and shops, but finally reaching the splendid center of Paris. There was the Seine River, laced with bridges; to the west she glimpsed the Eiffel Tower. It had been built only two years before for the World's Fair of 1889. It was the tallest structure in the world.

As Maria craned her neck eagerly, the horses trotted across the river, past the cathedral of Notre Dame, and up the Boulevard Saint-Michel. And there was the fabled university, a long white facade, more beautiful to Maria than any of the fairy-tale palaces in her sister Zosia's stories. Walking through the iron gates of the Sorbonne, Maria registered as a student in the Faculty of Science. She wrote her signature with the French version of her first name, "Marie."

There was so much for her to learn, from such brilliant teachers! Gabriel Lippmann, for instance, Professor of Experimental Physics and Director of the Research Laboratory. Or Henri Poincaré, a world-famous mathematician as well as a theoretical physicist. Professor Poincaré was a member of the prestigious French Academy of Sciences.

Before Marie could really make progress, though, she had to catch up. In spite of all her studying during the years at Szczuki, she was behind the other students in mathematics and chemistry. Also, to her embarrassment, she had a hard time understanding the lectures in French. She, who had been teaching French for years! Apparently she'd never learned the proper Parisian pronunciation herself. Besides, the professors at the Sorbonne spoke so rapidly.

On her way to Paris, Marie had worried about living with her sister Bronia and her brother-in-law Casimir, fearing that she might invade their privacy. She soon realized it would be the other way around. The Dluskis, both doctors, saw their patients at home, so people were continually coming and going during the day. Also, Casimir loved to have company, and he and Bronia had gathered a whole circle of Polish exiles. The house was often full of these interesting people: scientists, musicians, artists.

If Casimir wasn't expecting Marie to help him entertain their guests, he was dragging her out to a concert, the theater, or someone else's party. "I just want to stay in my room and study," she protested.

Once in a while Marie allowed herself to be lured away from her studies. During her first winter in Paris, she went to a patriotic Polish evening in a sculptor's loft. Part of the entertainment was the "living pictures" staged by the guests. Marie, with her blond hair loose on her shoulders, draped in the red of the Polish flag, posed as "Poland breaking her bonds." The Polish pianist Jan Paderewski played music by the Polish composer Chopin. The audience burst into applause.

Marie thought her father would like to hear that she'd taken a break from her studies, and she wrote him a description of the evening. But Mr. Sklodovski wrote back an anxious letter. There were Russian spies in Paris, he explained in careful words. They took down the names of any Poles who acted like Polish patriots. Those people were put on a blacklist, and if they came back to Warsaw—as Marie planned to do—they wouldn't be allowed to work there.

This incident made Marie realize that already she was taking the freedom of Paris for granted. How could she forget that she was banned from higher education in Warsaw? That was precisely why she'd traveled a thousand miles in order to study at a university.

Anyway, Marie wanted to give all her attention to her studies, not politics. After a few hectic months with the Dluskis, she moved to her own apartment. "I can't afford to take the streetcar to the university every day," she explained to Bronia. "And besides the cost of the fares, it takes time from my studies—an hour each way."

Marie's new home was just one tiny garret room, but it was in the Latin Quarter of Paris, where the students lived. It was within walking distance of the Sorbonne. Most importantly, here she could have some peace and quiet.

Shortly after Marie moved, Bronia and Casimir came over for tea. Bronia perched on Marie's only chair and sipped her tea from one of her three glasses. Casimir and Marie sat on the trunk, which also served as Marie's wardrobe.

"Oh, Manya," said her sister, looking around the drab, bare room. "Well, at least you have a fine view of Paris, up here in the attic."

Living on the sixth floor, Marie had to lug all her groceries and books up five flights of stairs. She also had to carry up the coal for the room's stove. But since she had to pay for her own coal, she didn't buy very much. She didn't buy many groceries, for that matter.

Marie spent most of her time at the lectures in the Sorbonne, in the laboratory, or in the library. The library was warm, and it was open until ten o'clock at night. Some of the other students met for parties or gathered in cafés, but Marie wasn't interested in socializing. She had been an eager learner ever since she was a little girl. Now, for the first time in her life, she could devote herself completely to studying.

She rose early and stayed up late. She hated to spend time or money on food, so she'd eat some bread with her tea and call it supper. She began to have dizzy spells, but she didn't worry. It only seemed natural to feel light-headed, existing in the thrilling realm of the mind.

Finally, though, Marie fainted in public, and some fellow students told Bronia and Casimir. Marie's brother-in-law marched her back to their apartment and made her eat a large, juicy steak. When Bronia came home, she took over.

"Casimir and I are both doctors, you know," scolded Bronia, "but it doesn't take a medical degree to guess that you've made yourself anemic. What would Papa say? We *order* you to eat and rest until your cheeks are pink again."

Marie didn't want to waste time taking care of herself, but even she could see the sense in it. After all, she had to stay well enough to study.

Gradually Marie made friends with a number of her fellow students, including Jadwiga Dydynska, another young Polish woman. Out of over 1,800 students, Marie and Jadwiga were among the mere twenty-three women enrolled in science courses.

In July 1893, Marie took her examination for her *licence es sciences*, similar to a master's degree in science. When the rankings were announced, she learned that she was first in her class. First of all of the students, after starting out so ill prepared, and struggling to understand the lectures!

Marie went back to Poland that summer to see her family, and then she returned to Paris to continue working toward her goal. Her friend Jadwiga Dydynska, well connected in Warsaw, used all her influence to make sure that Marie received a scholarship. That eased her money worries somewhat.

Even though Paris was such a paradise for learning, Marie didn't intend to stay there forever. She would study for three years, earning a degree in mathematics as well as in science. Then she would return to Warsaw, fully prepared to settle there, earn her living as a teacher, and dedicate her career to educating

Polish youth. And, of course, keep her promise to her father. Her brother Jozef and his wife were looking after Mr. Sklodovski for the time being, but Papa was counting on his Manya to join him as soon as she could.

One of the friends Marie made in Paris hoped to persuade her to stay. He was a Frenchman, Monsieur Lamotte. He admired her greatly, and he listened sympathetically to her ambitions. But when Marie realized that he hoped to marry her, she sadly said good-bye. Nothing was going to keep her from achieving her degree in mathematics and returning to Warsaw for good.

In the spring of 1894, Marie was studying hard for her mathematics examinations. Still, she couldn't help noticing that it was a beautiful time of year in Paris. Green leaves and grass brightened the landscape, and the chestnut trees were in bloom. A friend of Marie's, one of the few intelligent young women Marie had met in Szczuki, came to Paris on her honeymoon. Madame Kowalski, as she was called now, looked up Marie.

Her husband, Jozef Kowalski, was a professor of physics at the University of Freiburg. They were honeymooning in Paris because he'd been invited to lecture at the Sorbonne. Over tea at their boardinghouse, Marie told the Kowalskis about a project she was working on, in addition to studying for her degree in mathematics. She'd been hired by the French Society for the Encouragement of National Industry to compare the magnetic properties of different kinds of steel.

"The trouble is, I don't have enough laboratory space," Marie said. "Professor Lippmann kindly lets me share his laboratory at the Sorbonne, but I need more room to conduct my experiments."

"I believe I've met a man, a physicist, who would let you use part of his laboratory," said Jozef

Kowalski. "He's doing some work on magnetism at the Municipal School of Industrial Physics and Chemistry. He isn't well known in scientific circles, but in my opinion he's quite an original thinker."

So the next evening Marie came to the Kowalskis again, eager to talk to this physicist about laboratory space. When she stepped into the sitting room, a man was standing in front of the door to the balcony. He was tall and thin, with a full beard, dressed casually. His large eyes had a calm, dreamy expression.

"Marie Sklodovska," said Professor Kowalski, "may I present Pierre Curie?"

CHAPTER THIRTEEN

THE PERFECT MATCH

That first evening in the spring of 1894, Marie Sklodovska and Pierre Curie found a great deal to talk about. She explained her project of testing the magnetism in different steels, and she asked for his advice. He immediately offered her laboratory space.

Pierre described his work with his brother, Jacques, studying crystals. The Curie brothers had developed the piezoelectric quartz balance, which made it possible to measure tiny amounts of electric charge. As Pierre talked to Marie, he was impressed that she understood so quickly and asked such intelligent questions. At the same time, he was amazed that this brilliant, serious science student was also a beautiful young woman.

Marie was twenty-six. Pierre was thirty-five, though he looked much younger. He had never married. In his early twenties, he had fallen in love, but that young woman had been jealous of his passion for science. He longed for a woman who shared his dedication to his work, "a woman of genius," but he had given up trying to find her.

In France in the 1890s, not many men were looking for "a woman of genius." But Pierre, like Marie, had grown up in an unusual family. His parents, Eugène and Sophie-Claire Curie, had progressive ideas about educating their children. They realized that Pierre had an original mind and would not do well in conventional schools. They allowed him to develop in his own way.

Like the Sklodovskis, the Curies favored

progressive politics. Eugène, a doctor, had tended the wounded during the rebellions of 1848 and 1871 in Paris. The Curies had always taken Pierre and his brother, Jacques, to the countryside in the summer, so hiking, swimming, and studying nature had been as much a part of Pierre's childhood as Marie's.

In the weeks after their first meeting, Pierre called on Marie regularly. They talked eagerly about science and their work, agreeing that work was what made life joyful. Going on to talk about social and political matters, they found that they had a great deal in common there, too. For one thing, they both thought that scientific discoveries should be freely shared for the benefit of humanity. Both Pierre and Marie were teachers as well as learners, and they believed deeply in the importance of education.

As spring turned into summer, Marie studied hard to take the exams for her mathematics degree, her second degree from the Sorbonne. Meanwhile, Pierre and Marie continued to see each other. He sent her a copy of a paper he had just written, "On Symmetry in Physical Phenomena." "To Mlle. Sklodovska," he inscribed it, "with the respect and friendship of the author." Most young women would have preferred a bouquet of flowers or a box of candy, but Marie was much more pleased to share Pierre's work.

Marie passed her mathematics exams in July 1894 with high marks. Then she left for Poland, to spend the summer holidays with her family. Pierre, looking anxious and glum, saw her off at the train station. "I'm afraid I'll never see you again," he said as they waited on the platform. "Promise me that you'll come back to Paris in the fall."

"I don't know." Marie's voice trembled. "My father needs me, and he's getting old. And I'm Polish, don't you understand? I'm not free to do whatever I want. I have a duty to my native land!"

"I—" Pierre seemed to be on the verge of saying *I need you*, but he broke off and bowed his head. Then he went on, "I think you have a duty to develop your extraordinary mind. You can't study in your beloved Poland. Promise me that you'll come back to Paris to study! At least for one more year."

That summer Pierre sent Marie a stream of long letters. He wrote just the way he talked, and Marie could almost hear his voice as she read them. He told her about what he was doing and thinking, but he always came back to the same plea. "It would be a beautiful thing, a thing I dare not hope," he wrote, "if we could spend our life near each other hypnotized by our dreams. . . ."

"Oh, yes," Marie whispered to the page filled with Pierre's youthful scrawl. "It would be a beautiful thing." But what about her beloved

Poland? What about her dear family?

During the summer, feeling her father's fond gaze on her, Marie almost decided to settle down in Warsaw for good. She wrote back to Pierre, trying to explain her feelings.

But Pierre promptly sent another long letter back. "It would cause me great pain if you didn't come," he wrote bluntly. Besides, he argued, devoting her life to Poland was like smashing her head against a brick wall with the hope of breaking it down. "That might be an idea born of beautiful sentiments, but in fact this would be ridiculous and stupid."

Maybe he was right, thought Marie. For a hundred years Polish patriots had sacrificed their lives and talents—but Poland was still in chains. If Marie devoted her life to science, on the other hand, she might achieve something important for humanity.

"Papa," said Marie that afternoon as she poured his tea, "I love science as much as I love

Poland. And you're the one who taught me to love both of them. I need to learn more mathematics, but I can't study at the university in Poland. Listen, this is what Pierre Curie says." She read the part of Pierre's letter about the "brick wall." "What should I do?"

"Dear little Manya." Vladislav Sklodovski took the teacup from his daughter. "I think your friend Mr. Curie is right. You should return to Paris and study for a degree in mathematics."

"One more year, then," said Marie. She didn't tell her father about Pierre's plea to "spend our life near each other hypnotized by our dreams." She still wasn't sure what she would do about that. To Pierre's delight, Marie wrote back agreeing to return to Paris. She included a picture of herself in the letter, but she also had some practical questions. What did Pierre intend to live on in this hypnotic dream?

Pierre explained in his next letter that he would try to get a professorship, a better-paying position, at the School of Physics and Chemistry. He also suggested that Marie could teach at a normal school (a school for teachers), if she had French citizenship. He didn't quite say that Marie should marry him—but the obvious way for her to get French citizenship would be to become a Frenchman's wife.

Back in Paris that fall, Marie and Pierre drew closer and closer. She met his parents and his brother, and she immediately felt at home with them. In the spring of 1895, she wrote her family that she and Pierre were engaged. She was afraid they might be shocked and upset. In fact, they were happy for her, and they weren't a bit surprised.

On July 26, 1895, Marie Sklodovska and Pierre Curie were married in a civil ceremony in Sceaux, on the edge of Paris, where Pierre's parents lived. The bride was glowing, and she wore a brand-new dress. It was a navy-blue suit, which Marie chose because it would also be practical to wear in the laboratory.

Vladislav Sklodovski and Helena came from Warsaw for the wedding. The reception was held in Pierre's parents' garden, blooming with irises and roses. In a quiet moment with her father, Marie said, "Oh, Papa! I'm so happy. But it was so hard to decide to leave Warsaw—and you."

Her father squeezed her hand. "Hush, Manya. I can see that Pierre is truly your soul mate. You are meant to live and work together, just as your mother and I were. Nothing could give me more joy."

Marie's eyes blurred with tears, and she couldn't speak.

After the wedding, the newlywed couple left for a bicycling honeymoon in Brittany, on the northwest coast of France. Marie happily donned a bicycling outfit for ladies, which included knickers instead of the long skirt she usually wore.

Pierre Curie had never bothered to get a PhD, although he was doing original, important scientific work. But with Marie's encouragement he wrote his thesis and received his PhD in physics in March 1895, shortly before they were married. Pierre in turn encouraged Marie to work toward her own doctorate degree. But first she spent a year getting her teaching certificate. It was unusual at that time for middle-class women to work outside the home, but Marie had grown up expecting to earn her living. Besides, the Curies needed the money.

On September 12, 1897, Pierre and Marie's daughter Irène was born. Only two weeks later, Pierre's mother died of cancer. His father, Eugène Curie, moved in with the young family.

Among all these changes, Marie and Pierre never doubted that a life of scientific research, the "beautiful thing" that Pierre had proposed, was what they wanted. Sharing all their feelings and ideas, the Curies were charged with energy for their hard work. They felt lucky to be in the field of physics at such a thrilling time.

In 1895, the German scientist Wilhelm Roentgen had discovered X-rays. The world was astonished at the news that X-rays could peer inside the human body, producing pictures of the bones of living people on photographic plates. Then the French physicist Henri Becquerel had investigated the phosphorescence produced by X-rays. In the process, he accidentally discovered a mysterious energy released from uranium compounds. Becquerel reported his discovery, but he didn't try to find out more about it.

Because "Becquerel rays" were so new, Marie decided that investigating them would be a good subject for her doctoral thesis. On December 16, 1897, Marie began to keep a laboratory notebook on her doctoral research. Her "laboratory" was only a storeroom on the ground floor of the industrial school where Pierre taught.

"I'm afraid it will be damp and cold," Pierre apologized as he showed her the storeroom. "And it isn't furnished, except for those tables and that chair."

"But think of the advantages," Marie said cheerfully. "First, it's better than no laboratory at all. Second, you"—she gave him a kiss—"are working in the same building, so I can consult with you any time."

Within less than two months, the Curies had developed a way to measure the amount of "Becquerel rays" that a substance gave off. Marie used two sensitive instruments invented by Pierre and his brother, Jacques, some years before: the piezoelectric quartz balance and the precision electrometer. First she measured the electric current given off by uranium oxide.

Then, at random, she tried other substances: gold, copper—whatever samples she could beg from fellow researchers. None of these substances produced any rays.

Then Marie tested a sample of pitchblende, a mineral compound containing uranium. Surprisingly, it produced much more radiation than the uranium oxide alone. Marie went on to test other substances, and she discovered that the element thorium also gave off radiation. It seemed that uranium was not the only substance that produced "Becquerel rays." Pierre was so intrigued that he dropped his own research to work with her.

The Curies worked feverishly through March and the beginning of April 1898. Marie and Pierre suspected strongly that pitchblende contained not only uranium, but also some unknown element producing "Becquerel rays." Furthermore, Marie was beginning to think that this particular kind of radiation revealed something important about the atomic structure of elements.

Working harder than ever, the Curies satisfied themselves that they really had found a new radioactive element. They named it *polonium*, in honor of Marie's native land. Even in combination with bismuth, polonium gave off four hundred times as much of the mysterious radiation as uranium. The Curies coined a word, "radioactive," for these substances that produced "Becquerel rays." The term first appeared in print in the title of a paper they wrote describing their discoveries: "On a New Radio-Active Substance Contained in Pitchblende."

A few months later the Curies detected a second new element, which Pierre named "radium." In combination with barium, it was nine hundred times as radioactive as uranium.

Many other scientists were greatly impressed with the Curies' work, and that summer the French Academy of Science awarded Marie the Prix

Gegner. But she knew that she had not yet gathered enough proof for the scientific world at large. Science would accept the new elements only if they could examine them in their pure form, and if their exact atomic weights, the average mass of one atom, could be measured. And Marie wanted to do this, to satisfy her own perfectionism. Therefore, she set out to produce a sample of pure radium from pitchblende.

Marie and Pierre already knew that pitchblende contained only a tiny amount of radium. They estimated that the ore was, at most, 1 percent—one hundredth part—radium. So Marie would have to process a large amount of the ore to get a respectable sample of radium. Pitchblende had to be shipped all the way from the uranium mines in Bohemia (then under Austrian control, but now part of the Czech Republic). That much pitchblende would have been expensive, but the Austrian government allowed Marie to have the pitchblende residue, the ore from which the uranium had already been extracted.

Marie found a larger space to work, a wooden shed at Pierre's school. It contained a few wooden tables, a coal stove that barely functioned, and a blackboard. The day the pitchblende residue was delivered, Marie was so excited that she tore open one of the sacks and dug her hands into the ore. It was dull brown, mixed with pine needles, but to her it was more precious than a sack of gold.

Now began the really hard labor, stage after stage of extracting and refining the radium from the ore. In good weather, Marie worked outside the shed to avoid the poisonous fumes. Sometimes she spent all day watching a "boiling mass" in a cast-iron pot, stirring it with an iron rod.

Fortunately, Marie didn't realize at the beginning just how long and hard she would have to work. The amount of radium in pitchblende was not one-hundredth part, as she guessed, but one *millionth*. She would have to process a ton of the ore.

Marie's goal was to sort out the most radio-active ingredients of pitchblende and to keep refining them until she had a pure substance that was not uranium. When she had a pure sample of the new element, she would be able to prove it by the unique color lines it produced under spectroscopy. As Marie got closer to her goal, it became more and more important not to let her products become contaminated. But the "laboratory" shed, open for ventilation, was full of dirt and coal dust, causing Marie extra work to keep her samples pure.

The task of refining radium would take Marie almost four years of hard labor. It was exhausting, heroic work—exactly the kind of work Marie had always hoped to do. She was completely happy. And she shared her happiness with Pierre, who understood her perfectly. "He is a true gift of heaven," she wrote Bronia in 1899, "and the more we live together the more we love each other."

Marie and Pierre were both enchanted with their radioactive substances. Sometimes, after dark, they would walk the five blocks from their apartment to the laboratory and gaze at the luminous bluish silhouettes of the glass tubes and bottles. "Don't the glowing tubes look like fairy lights?" Marie asked Pierre.

In the fall of 1900, Marie began teaching at a girls secondary school, the École Normale Supérieure at Sèvres, a town on the outskirts of Paris. In spite of the time the school took away from her research, she enjoyed teaching. The physics students were all intelligent, hardworking girls, and she was eager to give them the all-important experience of laboratory work.

Even in her happiness, though, Marie missed her Polish family. Bronia and her husband, Casimir, had left Paris in 1898. They had moved to the Carpathian Mountains, in Austrian Poland, to open a sanitarium for tuberculosis patients. The next year, Marie and Pierre visited the sanitarium and met her father and her sisters for a reunion.

Marie was especially glad to see her old father in good health. But shortly after she returned to Paris, Vladislav Sklodovski was hit by a truck on the street in Warsaw. He was badly hurt, Jozef reported. For a while Marie wondered if she should make the long trip to Warsaw to see him, but then her father began writing letters again. He wanted to hear all about her progress, and he did not want her to stop work to visit him.

Toward the end of April 1902, after an exhausting but thrilling day, Marie sat down at the table to scribble a short letter to her father. "My dear Papa, what do you think? I have succeeded in isolating a decigram of pure salts of radium. That's a large enough sample to determine the atomic weight, so now I can write my doctoral dissertation with confidence." It had taken Marie five years to obtain a decigram, or .0035 ounces, of an ordinary-looking white powder: radium chloride.

Her father wrote back eagerly, "If you consider the amount of work that has been spent to obtain it, it is certainly the most costly of chemical elements!" His letter glowed with pride in his youngest daughter.

But shortly after her father's letter, Marie received another one from her brother. Their father had suffered a sudden gallbladder attack and he'd had surgery. However, Jozef thought he would recover well, and he urged her not to worry.

While Marie was wondering what to do, Jozef sent a telegram. Their father was not doing well after all, and he was not likely to live. Now Marie wanted to rush to Warsaw, but it took several hours just to clear her passport with the French authorities. The train trip itself took more than two days. Sadly, by the time she arrived, Vladislav Sklodovski had died.

Marie grieved that she hadn't been able to see her father one last time. On the other hand, she was thankful that he'd shared her excitement about her scientific discoveries. He had known, before he died, that she'd succeeded in isolating radium. She could now determine the atomic weight of radium and announce its place in Mendeleev's periodic table of the elements.

The original goal of Marie's research, back in 1897, had been to earn her PhD. After producing the sample of radium, she finally turned to writing her dissertation. The scientific community understood that Marie's discoveries about radioactivity were an important breakthrough, and her dissertation was published in England as well as France.

In June 1903, Marie defended her doctoral dissertation in the students' hall at the Sorbonne. Sunlight poured through the tall windows on Marie, at the front of the hall, wearing the new dress Bronia had talked her into buying. The dress was dark gray, a nice practical color for laboratory work.

As Marie described her research in a low, confident voice, the audience beamed with pride. Pierre, his father, and Marie's sister Bronia from Poland were there, as well as Marie's admiring physics students from the teacher's preparatory school at Sèvres. The three examiners, including Marie's former professor Gabriel Lippmann, knew and respected her work, and there was no question that they would award her the degree of doctor of physical science. She was the first woman to receive a doctorate from the Sorbonne.

Paul Langevin, a former student of Pierre's, invited the Curies and their family to a celebration dinner that night. The New Zealand physicist Ernest Rutherford, who happened to be in Paris, was also included. Rutherford was studying uranium rays, and he was intensely interested in the Curies' work.

After dinner Pierre announced, "I have something to show you all. Come into the garden, please!" When the guests were gathered in the dark garden, he took a test tube from his pocket.

"Aah," they exclaimed at its magical blue glow.

"That, my friends," Pierre declared, "is a solution of radium."

Marie smiled at her husband, as excited as a child with a wonderful new toy. When they were back in the drawing room, however, Rutherford spoke to her in a quiet voice. "My dear Madame Curie, aren't you concerned about the dangers of handing this radium of yours? I couldn't help noticing how badly cracked Pierre's fingers are."

"Oh, yes, I am a little concerned," Marie answered, but she smiled as if to underline "little." She held out her own sore, cracked fingertips. "It's the price of working in a laboratory, eh?"

The discovery of two new elements was stunning, but more important was what radioactivity revealed about the atom. Before this, many physicists did not even believe that atoms—particles too small to be seen with the microscopes of the time—were the basic building blocks of all matter. They had been even more skeptical when J. J. Thomson, an English physicist, had proposed his explanation of cathode rays in 1897. Thomson thought that cathode rays, the beams of light between the negative and positive anodes in a vacuum tube, were actually a stream of subatomic particles that he called "electrons."

Even scientists who accepted the concept of atoms did not believe that the atom could be further divided. Mendeleev, the creator of the periodic table, argued vigorously against Thomson's ideas. But as radioactive elements were studied, it became clear that they were giving off particles from their atoms because their atomic weight decreased over time.

In November 1903, Marie and Pierre Curie were informed that they, along with Henri Becquerel, had won the Nobel Prize for physics. Strange as it seems now, some prominent French scientists had tried to have Marie shut out of the prize. Marie's former professor Gabriel Lippmann was one of them, although he had followed the progress of her research and even raised money for her. They nominated only Pierre Curie and Becquerel, describing the discovery of radium and polonium as if Pierre alone had accomplished it. When Pierre heard about the nomination, he declared that he "wished to be considered together with Madame Curie."

Fortunately several other top scientists, including the Swedish physicist Knut Angstrom, acknowledged the truth about Marie's accomplishments. They lobbied for her and won. And so Marie Sklodovska Curie became the first woman to receive a Nobel Prize.

The prize was awarded to Henri Becquerel and Pierre and Marie Curie for "their joint researches on the radiation phenomena." Still, in newspaper articles Marie was usually described as Pierre's helper. Most people could not accept the idea that a wife could be an equal partner with her husband.

Pierre was also elected to the prestigious French Academy of Sciences and given a professor's position at the Sorbonne. Now the Curies were famous, although neither of them wanted to be. Just the opposite: They were horrified to be visited by reporters and photographers who wanted to know all about their personal lives.

Sometimes the journalists invented details

that they thought their readers would enjoy. An article in *la Patrie* quoted Marie on the fact that Pierre had been elected to the French Academy of Sciences but she had not: "Oh! Me, I am only a woman." Marie had never said anything like that in her life. She immediately wrote a letter to *la Patrie*, denying the quotation.

The Curies received an avalanche of mail, including a letter from an American who wanted permission to name his racehorse after Marie. They did not answer such letters.

What the Curies wanted, instead of becoming celebrities, was to be given a well-equipped laboratory and a steady income. They longed to be left alone, to spend all their time continuing their research. "So this is fame," Marie commented to Pierre late one evening at home. They were both bone-weary, and yet another uninvited autograph-seeker had just left. "What a disaster!"

Between laboratory work and teaching, Marie

and Pierre didn't have much time to spend with their daughter, Irène. Marie was grateful that her father-in-law, Eugène Curie, was part of their household. The tall, old man with white hair and bright blue eyes was a devoted grandfather. He delighted in sharing his love of nature and science with Irène, as he had with Pierre at the same age. Irène and her grandfather had a special close relationship.

In 1904, when Irène was seven, the Curies' second daughter, Ève, was born. Meanwhile, Marie had become worried about Pierre's health. His hands now hurt so much that it was hard for him to get dressed. He had lost his old energy, and he suffered from pain in his legs and back.

In spite of early signs of danger, the Curies refused to admit how harmful their cherished radioactive elements might be. Pierre had actually experimented with a sample of radioactive barium, fastening it to his arm for ten hours.

He received a burn that took several weeks to heal. Now the Curies were both run down and losing weight. Marie's fingertips, too, had grown hard and painful. But they both blamed their worrisome symptoms on overwork.

Still, the Curies were supremely happy together. One warm day in April 1906, they took a trip to the countryside near Paris. Marie would always remember that day. She and Pierre stretched out to rest in a meadow, and he stroked her hair. Ève toddled through the grass and Irène chased butterflies.

On April 19, the Curies were back at work in Paris. That day Pierre spoke enthusiastically at a luncheon meeting of the newly formed Association of Professors of the Science Faculties. Afterward, in the pouring rain, he walked from the meeting toward the Institut de France, where he intended to use the library.

Crossing a busy intersection with his umbrella up, Pierre probably didn't notice the heavy wagon rumbling down on him. The wagon driver didn't see Pierre until the moment he appeared from behind a carriage. It was impossible for the wagon to stop. A wheel struck Pierre's head and killed him instantly.

And so Marie's husband, her "true gift of heaven," was snatched away from her by a senseless accident. The joy of living and working with her soul mate in perfect harmony was over. Marie was crushed with grief. Her pain was so intense that she couldn't talk to anyone about it. She wrote in her journal, "I repeat your name again and always 'Pierre, Pierre, Pierre, my Pierre,' alas that doesn't make him come back, he is gone forever, leaving me nothing but desolation and despair."

CHAPTER FOURTEEN

THE NOBEL PRIZE WINNER

On November 5, 1906, at the age of almost thirty-nine, Marie Curie gave her first lecture at the Sorbonne. She had been appointed a professor of physics in Pierre's place. She was the first woman ever allowed to teach at the Sorbonne, since its founding in the twelfth century.

A curious audience crammed the small amphitheater where Pierre had given his last physics lecture. They filled the corridors and even the square outside the science building. Many of them had no interest in science; they were hoping to hear the slender, blond widow pour out her grief for her famous husband.

But Marie did not satisfy their curiosity.

Stepping up to the demonstration table at the front of the hall, she began to lecture about recent developments in physics. It was agonizing for Marie to take Pierre's place in the School of Physics, but she was determined that their work would go on. She knew how proud and joyful Pierre would have been, seeing her at last a professor at the Sorbonne.

Sometimes, when worrying about the future, Marie would say to Pierre that if she didn't have him, she probably wouldn't work anymore. He had told her it was wrong to speak that way, and that "it was necessary to continue no matter what." But then he admitted that if he lost her, he would be "nothing more than a body without a soul." Still, he thought he would go on working. He was right, Marie felt now, and teaching was a way for her to stay close to him.

Marie also carried on from her strong sense of duty, and because she loved her two children and their grandfather, Eugène Curie. In the spring of 1907, she moved the family from Paris to Sceaux, where Pierre had grown up. Outside the city, there would be room for Irène and Ève to play outdoors. Marie had a gym set with a trapeze, rings, and a climbing rope put up for the children. Like her own parents, she believed in physical as well as mental education for her children.

Pierre and Marie both disapproved of conventional schooling, and they wanted something better for their daughters. Now Marie, along with a few other parents, began an alternative school. This school encouraged children to explore and think for themselves, and to develop their bodies as well as their minds. Marie believed that science education should combine a love of nature with the urge to understand nature. That was Vladislav Sklodovski's approach, and it had first sparked Marie's fascination with science. Now the Curie family spent their summer vacations at the seaside, where they swam and bicycled and enjoyed the natural world.

Both of Marie's daughters were talented, although in different ways. Irène, a high achiever in mathematics and science, took after her mother and father. Ève, on the other hand, seemed to have inherited her aunt Helena's musical talent. The pianist Jan Paderewski, a family friend, heard Ève play the piano at the age of six and was impressed.

Meanwhile, Marie threw herself into her work as fiercely as ever. She wrote her "Treatise on Radioactivity," which summed up brilliantly all the research to date. Most of the time she was at the laboratory or the lecture hall rather than at home.

One of the friends who shared Marie's grief over Pierre Curie's death was Paul Langevin. He was also a physicist, a former student of Pierre's, and he had taught with Marie at the school for teachers at Sèvres. Pierre and Marie had both admired Langevin's intelligence and his research work. Now Marie was glad for his friendship. She and her girls took a summer vacation with Paul Langevin, his wife, and their children in 1908.

With Pierre gone, Marie was more grateful than ever for her father-in-law. While he mourned deeply for his son, he was not overwhelmed the way Marie was. He played with the children, read them poetry, and exchanged funny letters with Irène. In fact, he took the place of a parent for them. But only a few years after his son Pierre's death, Eugène Curie became ill. He died in February 1910. Irène, closer to her grandfather than to anyone else, took his death especially hard.

During that spring, Marie's friendship with Paul Langevin developed into a romantic attachment. Langevin was deeply unhappy in his marriage, and Marie thought that he should leave his wife. She hoped that with Paul, she could again have a marriage of minds and hearts, as she had with Pierre.

In mid-September, 1910, Marie Curie traveled to Brussels, Belgium, for the International Congress of Radiology and Electricity. Ernest Rutherford, from the University of Manchester in England, also attended. Unfortunately, Marie wasn't able to participate fully in the meeting, because she was ill most of the time. But the congress gave her the commission of preparing a sample of pure radium, which would be the international standard for that element. The unit of measurement, they decided, would be called a "curie," in honor of Pierre.

Back in Paris, friends of Marie were eager to nominate her to the prestigious French Academy of Sciences. She would have been made a member some time ago, as Pierre had been, if she hadn't been a woman. She had already been elected a member of the Swedish, Dutch, Czech, Polish, and Russian academies.

But the French academy had never admitted a woman in 250 years, and many of its members did not want to start now.

Besides, French society in general disapproved of women who pursued careers in "masculine" fields such as science. When the news came out that Marie Curie was a nominee for the Academy of Sciences, there was a public outcry. Many respected people, including women, wrote protests in the press. The Academy itself was in an uproar.

When the vote was finally taken in January 1911, Marie Curie was rejected. Instead, the Academy of Sciences elected Edouard Branly, an older physicist who had made an important contribution to the invention of the radio. The Curies' friend Charles Guillaume wrote Marie angrily, "The election of M. Branly was achieved by methods which would embarrass monkeys."

All Marie's friends were indignant for her.

But if Marie cared, she didn't complain. And her accomplishments spoke for themselves, with or without the Academy's approval. After four years of dogged labor, she had produced a sample of pure radium metal. It was a brilliant white. Marie also felt hopeful about her personal life, because Paul Langevin had left his wife.

In November 1911, Marie Curie and Paul Langevin traveled to Brussels to attend the Solvay Conference in Physics. There, they met Albert Einstein, who liked Langevin but was especially taken with Marie Curie's "sparkling intelligence." Marie and Einstein would become good friends.

Unfortunately, as the Solvay Conference closed, a public scandal broke in Paris. Paul Langevin's wife was not about to let him go peaceably, and she told the press about her husband's affair. All the newspapers were full of the story: The famous physicist Marie Curie was romantically involved with Paul Langevin, a married man with four children.

Langevin's wife blamed Marie for the breakup of their marriage, although the Langevins had been miserable almost from their wedding day. Most of French society also blamed Marie. The French press called her "this foreign woman," "the husband-stealer," and "a feminist."

Meanwhile, the Nobel Chemistry Committee had decided to award Marie Curie the Nobel Prize in Chemistry for 1911. She deserved this award, they noted, for establishing the atomic weight for radium and for producing radium in a metallic state. It was a momentous honor, and Marie should have been a national hero. But public opinion in Paris was violently against her, and so the Paris papers hardly mentioned Madame Curie's second Nobel Prize.

Marie's scientist friends, including Albert Einstein and Marie's brother-in-law, Jacques Curie, supported her. But all during November, the public scandal grew. Paul Langevin fought a duel with a magazine editor over the insults the man had published. At the end of the month, Marie received a letter from the Nobel Committee in Sweden. They asked her *not* to come to Stockholm to receive her Nobel Prize.

Marie wrote back crisply, "In fact the prize has been awarded for the discovery of Radium and Polonium. I believe that there is no connection between my scientific work and the facts of private life." Therefore, she said, she planned to come to Sweden to accept the prize.

As for Paul Langevin, he couldn't make up his mind to divorce his wife, even though they were so unhappy. He and Marie remained friends, but their romance ended.

Marie Curie was too proud and independent to live her life to please public opinion, but at the same time, the strain of the public scandal was too much for her. After returning from the award ceremonies in Stockholm, she fell ill.

On December 29, Marie was taken to the hospital. It was found that she suffered from a serious kidney disease, and in March 1912, she had surgery. For the next year or so she hardly worked at all. She visited one spa after another, trying to recover her health.

At the same time, Marie eagerly followed the ongoing developments in the field of radioactivity. She and Albert Einstein wrote back and forth about Max von Laue's research on gamma rays, one of the types of radiation given off by radium. In March of 1913, Einstein and his wife visited Marie in Paris. By the time of the Solvay Conference in October 1913, Marie was well enough to attend.

There was an ongoing controversy among physicists about the structure of the atom. J. J. Thomson, who had first proposed that cathode rays were streams of subatomic particles, thought the atom was made up of a "jelly" of positive electric charge. The tiny negatively charged electrons and larger positively charged alpha particles were embedded in the jelly, he suggested.

Ernest Rutherford disagreed, because this model didn't explain the results of all the new research, including Niels Bohr's. Rutherford proposed that the atom was more like a solar system, with the electrons orbiting a positively charged core or nucleus. Most of the physicists at the Solvay Conference of 1913 ignored Rutherford's idea, but Marie thought he had hit on something important.

In November 1913, Marie Curie was invited to Warsaw. A radium institute had been built there in her honor, and she was asked to dedicate it. During the celebrations, Marie revisited the Museum of Industry and Agriculture, where she had done her first laboratory work almost twenty-four years ago. At a banquet, she met Jadwiga Sikorska, the director of young Manya Sklodovska's school, and she kissed the old lady affectionately. Marie also visited the Powazki cemetery and the family tomb where her father, her mother, and her sister Zosia rested.

When World War I broke out in August 1914, Marie Curie was at work in Paris. Unlike many who thought the war would be over in a few weeks, Marie was sure that Europe was in for a terrible massacre. Still, she hoped to make a contribution to France's war effort. "You and I, Irène," she wrote her older daughter, "we will try to make ourselves useful."

That summer Irène and Ève Curie were vacationing with a governess and housekeeper on the coast of Brittany. Irène, age seventeen, planned to enroll at the Sorbonne in the fall. Her ambition was to work as a partner with her mother in the laboratory.

Marie quickly hit on the idea of taking the new medical technology of X-rays to wounded French soldiers. She was the ideal person to make this happen. She knew a great deal about the medical field, since her brother, Jozef, and her sister Bronia were both doctors. She had followed the study of X-rays from the time of Roentgen's first discovery, and she understood X-ray equipment. Most important, she was fiercely dedicated to any task she undertook.

Marie designed and had built "radiology cars," X-ray vans equipped with their own source of electricity as well as the equipment to perform X-rays on patients. She not only put together the medical technology, but also raised the money to pay for it. Then, the hardest part: She convinced French government and military officials how helpful this brandnew method could be. By November 1914, Marie and Iréne were allowed to set out for the front in a radiology car.

As well as operating an X-ray station herself, Marie trained technicians and surgeons to use the new techniques. She raised more money and set up a school to train nurses and other women as X-ray technicians. Irène also became one of the teachers at this school. Although only eighteen by this time, Irène was extremely intelligent and well educated, and she had the cool mind needed in emergency situations.

After four years of terrible slaughter (France alone lost more than a million men), World War I ended on November 11, 1918. The next year, at the Treaty of Versailles, the nation of Poland was granted independence. At least one great joy, thought Marie Sklodovska Curie, had come out of all that suffering. Poland, after more than a century of domination by Imperial Russia and other powers, was a free country.

CHAPTER FIFTEEN

LIKE A FAIRY TALE

Pierre and Marie Curie had always agreed that the ideas and research results of science ought to be free for anyone, instead of being used for private gain or national interests. After the Curies discovered radium, they had refused to patent their process for preparing the element. By not doing so they had bypassed the chance to make a fortune.

After World War I, Marie Curie became more and more convinced that scientists around the world should join together and share their knowledge. Although she hated to spend time working on anything except laboratory research and teaching, Marie made an exception in one case. She served on the

Commission on Intellectual Cooperation of the League of Nations, the newly formed organization to promote world peace.

But Marie's passion and most of her time went into running the Pavillon Curie, a laboratory for research in radioactivity. The University of Paris had promised Pierre a really fine new laboratory when they made him a professor of physics. Construction of the laboratory was finally begun, with Marie's urging, in 1912.

In the Curie laboratory in Paris, Marie made a point of hiring talented women, which was highly unusual for the time. She also invited many scientists to come from other countries—places as far away as China. In 1918, Irène started helping her mother run the laboratory and began conducting her own research.

At work, Marie always looked the same: a slight, intense woman in a stained laboratory coat. She never wanted to spend money on furnishings or clothes for herself. When her daughter Ève managed to get her into a clothing shop, Marie would only point to the simplest dress—black, of course—and the cheapest hat. As her friend Albert Einstein remarked, "Marie Curie is, of all celebrated beings, the only one whom fame has not corrupted."

But for her research, on the other hand, Marie craved nothing but the best. She was willing to make a pest of herself at government ministries or to butter up private donors in order to get generous funding. In 1921, in spite of her dislike of traveling to new places, Marie decided to visit the United States. The idea for the visit came from Missy Meloney, an American journalist and magazine editor who admired Marie and wanted to do something to help her work.

After coming to Paris to meet Marie, Missy launched a publicity campaign in the United States. The purpose was to raise the money—$100,000—to buy a gram of radium for Marie's research. Within a year Missy had raised the funds, mainly from alumni of women's colleges such as Smith, Vassar, Wellesley, and Bryn Mawr. Marie agreed to come to the United States to accept the gift personally.

Marie's ocean liner docked in New York in May 1921. Americans were surprised that the heroic Madame Curie was a "motherly looking scientist" in a plain black dress, as the *New York Times* described her. Marie was surprised by the monthlong round of ceremonies, luncheons, dinners, and meetings that she was expected to attend, always as the guest of honor. Her tour included several women's colleges and Harvard and Yale. By the time she reached the White House, where President Warren Harding welcomed her, her arm was in a sling from too much handshaking.

Marie Curie was not well, suffering from low blood pressure, dizziness, and anemia. She had to cancel several of the events planned for her visit. Irène and Ève, on the other hand, enjoyed themselves greatly, especially in the West. But in the end, Marie was greatly satisfied to leave the United States at the end of June with the precious gift, one gram of radium.

After her return to France, Marie wrote a biography of Pierre Curie, published in 1923. "I hope," she wrote in the preface, ". . . that it will help to conserve his memory. I wish, too, that it might remind those who knew him of the reasons for which they loved him." She included a few pages of "Autobiographical Notes," ending with a description of her trip to America and the generosity of Americans. She wrote this part in English, and it wasn't printed in the French edition of Pierre's biography.

At that time, there were great hopes that radium might be a miracle cure for cancer. In fact, radium treatment was successful in curing some malignant tumors. Since radioactivity harmed quickly growing cancer cells more than normal cells, it could be used to destroy only malignant tissue. Research on the medical uses of radium would eventually lead to the development of radiation therapy, an important treatment for certain types of cancers.

But the evidence was mounting up that exposure to radioactive materials was dangerous, and not only because it burned the skin. In factories where watch dials were painted with radium paint to make them glow in the dark, many workers had sickened and died. The researchers in laboratories and the medical personnel who handled X-ray equipment or radium for medical therapy suffered anemia, leukemia, and the loss of fingers, arms, or eyes.

Marie's laboratory took more precautions than most, but even so some of her workers became ill and died of radiation poisoning. Marie herself must have been extremely resistant to radiation, considering that she had worked with pitchblende unprotected for years. Now she refused to admit that her chronic ailments, as well as the cataracts in her eyes, were caused by radiation.

In spite of her ailments, Marie had no intention of retiring. As ever, she was happiest in the laboratory, caught up in a dreamlike state in which she forgot to be hungry or tired. Speaking at a conference in Spain in 1933, Marie Curie explained how she experienced her scientific work: "A scientist in his laboratory is not only a technician: he is also a child placed before natural phenomena which impress him like a fairy tale."

Irène Curie had grown up to be her mother's partner, just as they had both wanted. Like Marie, Irène was happiest at work in the laboratory. In 1926, when she was twenty-nine, Iréne married a fellow scientist, Frederic Joliot, who also worked in the Curie laboratory. Like Pierre and Marie Curie, the Joliot-Curies shared a passion for scientific research. Their important work with polonium led to the discovery of the neutron, another subatomic particle, by a laboratory in England.

On January 15, 1934, Irène and Frederic Joliot-Curie discovered that radioactive elements could be produced by artificial means. They proudly showed their product, an unstable radioactive isotope of phosphorus in a test tube, to Marie. Her eyes shone with joy as she took the glass tube in her own radium-burned fingers. She held up a Geiger counter, an instrument for measuring radioactivity, to test the substance.

The next year, Irène and Frederic would receive the Nobel Prize in Chemistry for their achievement. But in the meantime, Marie finally became too ill to work. On July 4, 1934, she died of leukemia, a disease of the blood that can be caused by radiation exposure. She was sixty-seven.

In a simple, private ceremony, Marie was buried in the same grave with Pierre in Sceaux. Bronia and Jozef came from Poland for the funeral. Each of them brought a handful of Polish soil to drop on her coffin.

Marie Curie's daughters honored their mother with their careers, each in her own way. In December 1935, Irène and Frederic Joliot-Curie went to Stockholm to receive the Nobel Prize in Chemistry. Irène was the second woman, after Marie Curie, to be awarded a Nobel Prize in the physical sciences.

Ève not only was gifted musically, she was also a talented writer. After Marie's death, Ève decided to write her mother's biography. She was determined to tell the story of this extraordinary woman she knew and loved before anyone else came out with a biography full of misinformation. In 1937, Ève's book, *Madame Curie*, was published. It was translated into many languages, and it is still in print.

★ ★ ★ ★

Marie Curie was one of the great scientific minds of the nineteenth and twentieth centuries. In her discovery of polonium and radium, she realized the most important thing about the new elements. That is, she saw that radioactivity was an "atomic property." The study of radioactivity revealed that the atom was not, after all, the indivisible unit of matter. And so science's concept of the nature of the atom began to change.

Marie also proved what a gifted woman could accomplish in science, a field that had been almost completely closed to women. As a dedicated teacher, she brought along many women scientists, including her daughter Iréne, and they went on to achievements of their own. Marie Curie's very name is still an inspiration to women who dream of great accomplishments.

FOR MORE INFORMATION

VIDEOS

From Alchemy to the Atom.
By Robert Raymond; Michael Charlton.
Opus Films; PBS Video; PBS Adult
Learning Service.
Published by PBS Video, 1983.

On the Banks of the Niemen.
Based on the novel by Eliza Orzeszkowa.
Directed by Zbigniew Kuzminski, 1987.
Polart Distribution, ©2003.
This movie, based on a book by one of Marie
Curie's favorite authors, gives a good idea of
Polish country life and the Polish patriotic
spirit at the time of Marie's youth.

BOOKS

Curie, Ève. *Madame Curie*. Garden City, NY: Doubleday, 1937.

An affectionate, highly readable biography, by Marie Curie's younger daughter.

Pflaum, Rosalynd. *Marie Curie and Her Daughter Irène*. Minneapolis, MN: Lerner Publications, 1993.

Brief but good. Black-and-white photographs are of high quality.

ON THE INTERNET

http://www.aip.org/history/curie/contents.htm
An exhibit on Marie Curie's life and work, offered by The Center for History of Physics, of The American Institute of Physics.

http://www.curie.fr/fondation/musee/visite-virtuelle.cfm/lang/_gb.htm

The Web page of the Institut Curie in Paris.

http://www.ptchem.lodz.pl/en/museum.
html#InsideMuseum1
The Web site of the Maria Sklodowska Curie
Museum in Warsaw.
Gives a brief virtual tour of the exhibits.

FOR ADULT READERS

Brian, Denis. *The Curies: A Biography of the Most Controversial Family in Science.* Hoboken, NJ: Wiley, 2005.

Quinn, Susan. *Marie Curie: A Life.* Reading, MA: Addison-Wesley, 1995.
An up-to-date (includes letters and papers not released until the 1990s), thorough, and highly regarded biography.